EXPERT TO
INFLUENCER

JANE ANDERSON

Copyright © Jane Anderson 2017

ISBN 978-0-648-04890-9

All rights reserved. No part of this book may be reproduced or transmitted in any form or by any means, electronic or mechanical, including photocopying (except under the statutory exceptions provisions of the Australian Copyright Act 1968), recording, scanning or by any information storage and retrieval system without the prior permission of the publisher.

Cover design, internal design and copy editing: Lauren Shay – Full Stop Writing, Editing and Design.

"I love Jane's work, and I love who she is as a person. She takes her own medicine – her profile is ranked in the top 1% of LinkedIn worldwide and Feedspot recently rated her blog at #22 in the top 100 most influential branding blogs globally. She's my go-to person for any thought leader who needs to improve their brand and needs to get in front of people in a new market. She's also the person who supports me around my profile and branding – I feel very fortunate to be her client. More than that, she's an inspiring person who is a pleasure to work with. Not only is she the best in Australia at what she does, she's generous, straight, and brings joy to her work."
– Peter Cook, CEO, Thought Leaders Business School

"The speed of change in business is happening faster than ever. Any service-based industry with formal qualifications such as hairdressing means being an Influencer is now imperative. Having the skills to market yourself is the new black. This book from Jane will set you up with the skills for future-proofing your career. Jane will teach you the recipe for how to position yourself and your brand to set yourself up for success. This book (along with all of Jane's other books, too!) has been the best investment I've ever made into my business."
– Tracey Hughes CSP, Hairdressing Expert & Global Educator, 8 x Educator of the Year, 10 x Salon of the Year, 2 x Hairdresser of the Year, Australian Masters Inductee

"Within four weeks of making a couple of modest tweaks, Jane Anderson's advice led to me increasing online revenue by more than 10 times! Simple, clear, direct strategies that increase impact and influence."
– Dr Justin Coulson, Parenting Expert

"It's now four days into the new month and I have only three days of availability left to book in. On top of that, my average sale has increased between 25% to 100%. And that is not from simply increasing prices, it's from being able to communicate with my clients on what services I can provide to them, it's educating them on what is best for their business and on how to leverage their time and investment with me."
– Kerrin Smith, Photography expert

"Jane Anderson is the go-to expert for building your personal brand. She helps leaders and business owners transform their relationship with social media from one of awkwardness to that of a powerful business-building ally."
– Dan Gregory, CEO of the Impossible Institute, regular guest on ABC's Gruen Transfer

"After establishing a consultancy a few years ago, I felt my brand needed to mature to take into account the shift in my client base and my own expertise. Plus, I was too close to my own material and blind to my own weak points. Jane was empathetic, yet effective, and her knowledge of marketing and lead generation for thought leaders and Influencers is second to none. With just a few sessions, I have repositioned myself in the marketplace and created a whole new range of offerings that will enable me to have far bigger impact."
- **Amanda Blesing, Women and Diversity Expert**

"I'd just like to first thank you again for the fantastic couple of days in the Lead Generation Workshop. It's given me the structure, tools and processes to help move my practice forward. There's still a lot of work to do, but I'm feeling much more confident about how to get it all done to drive my practice forward. As a green belt, it was exactly the sort of insights I needed. Thank you."
- **James Anderson, Growth Mindset Expert**

"Jane is an extraordinary thought leader. Her work on presence and impact helps us stay real and connected in a crazy online world. Jane is the real deal – her work is measured and substantial. Anyone trying to create and demonstrate a point of difference would benefit from working with Jane and her team."
- **Matt Church, Founder, Thought Leaders Business School, Top 10 Speakers Globally**

"If you feel like you are not getting the traction from social media and you know that there must be more to it, it is time to tap into Jane Anderson's phenomenal insights. Jane delivers practical, tested strategies that work. She has tremendous knowledge and a deep understanding of how to build a meaningful network and personal brand that matters."
- **Dan Diamond, Resilience Expert, TEDx Speaker, Winner of the Barack Obama The President's Volunteer Service Award**

"Jane Anderson is full of wisdom, insights and practical tips for people who are serious about taking control of their professional brand."
- **Gabrielle Dolan, Storytelling Expert, Bestselling Author**

"Jane presented at a group of Australia's best speakers on how to maximise your return on LinkedIn. While I thought I knew how to use LinkedIn, Jane took this to another level. The key element was the strategy behind how to maximise my time using it rather than clicking and posting madly with little or no results. From her presentation, I can see why Jane is having such a significant impact on the marketplace with her work. If you want to progress your business using LinkedIn then you MUST get Jane on board."
- **Warwick Merry, National President, Professional Speakers Association**

"This session inspired me to completely recreate my professional resume, LinkedIn and clean up my social identity. Jane has given me the confidence to believe in myself and all my career and university achievements, and to stop letting others tell me what I can and can't be proud of. Thank you so much, Jane. You have really opened my eyes up to the opportunities that I am able to achieve!"
– Chloe McGurgan, Talent and Culture Manager, Accor Hotels

"Jane is an exceptional facilitator, presenter and coach for executives and senior managers. She works closely with our Learning & Development team at Sunsuper to deliver a range of development programs in leadership, personal branding, and personal and professional effectiveness, and she always delivers outstanding results."
– Leanne Whicker, HR Director, Sunsuper

"Jane is a refreshing and contemporary expert on all things 'presence'. Whether it's your branding, your LinkedIn profile and optimising its use or how you are perceived in your market, her intellectual property, born from extensive experience, makes her stuff just 'pop'! It's clear, insightful and a bit of a game changer when it comes to getting noticed for the right things – no matter your field or industry."
– Lynne Cazaly, Creativity and Innovation Expert

"Jane is an outstanding and motivational trainer, very thorough in her preparation and exceptional in her delivery. She has a special gift for sharing her passions with people, particularly with customer-service skills, interpersonal skills, and preparing people to take the next step in their careers. I thoroughly recommend Jane as a trainer, facilitator and coach."
– Fiona Loughlan, Executive Leader

"Jane is one of the most professional and nicest persons I know. Jane is not only generous in advice but also her time and shares her experience and expertise willingly. This is combined with an ability to really listen to her clients' needs and adopt a collaborative approach to tailor a profile or adapt a specific requirement. Jane ensures that she achieves optimal and high-quality outcomes for her clients and truly believes in the success of others. Jane really stands out as a person of true altruism, committed and sincere in all her undertakings. I would highly recommend Jane."
– Tania Wyngaard, Talent Management Expert, UQ Business School MBA Program

"If you are wanting to get traction with your business growth, lead generation and LinkedIn, there is no better person than Jane Anderson. She is a complete thought leader in this space and even better, she acts and lives her recommendations and is a beautiful, generous person with it. She takes you from ideas to action super-fast! I am in awe of Jane's drive, willingness to share and leverage everything for impact. Jane truly connects and makes impact. She is a world leader and an amazing, inspirational woman. I recommend you connect with Jane – your business and life will be better for it."
– Kelly Tomney, Personal Branding and Employer Branding Expert

"Over the past six months, I have had the pleasure of watching Jane in action as a thought leader … and a very special thought leader she is. Hence, I have become one of Jane's clients, implementing her LinkedIn strategy. I found her expertise and knowledge very beneficial to my own business and myself. I recommend her highly as she is a very practical and genuine professional who commits completely to her clients and her network. Jane goes that 'extra mile', making her so unique."
– Gail Stevens, Mortgage Broking Expert

"Jane's experience and knowledge shine through in her ability to connect, de-clutter and shape the way we work online. Not only is she a wonderful, positive presence and a joy to work with, her vision and drive make it all the more engaging. She creates a real impact for those she works with and for."
– Nikki Fogden-Moore, Vitality Expert, Top 100 Women on Influence

"Jane is one of the most valuable speakers on lead generation and the value of LinkedIn. I had the pleasure of hearing her speak last year – she was clear, practical and gave insights into the power of LinkedIn. I subsequently bought her book *CONNECT* and have implemented many of her recommendations. The result: a significant increase in my global network within my industry, which has led to valuable working relationships. I post with more confidence and have had exponential engagement with my network."
– Andrea Shepperson, Dental Expert

"If you have realised that YOU are a business of one and that your brand must be managed with the care and attention that any good business deserves, then Jane Anderson is for you. In fact, Jane's success as one of the leading advisers on personal branding is because she is focused on your success. I have found her practical suggestions and thoughtful advice to be enormously valuable. I highly recommend Jane if you would like to take your brand to another level with your target market."
– Brian Donovan, Leadership Expert

"Jane's expertise in raising your personal profile regarding social media, specifically LinkedIn, has been amazing. After recently attending an information session that Jane was running, I was amazed at how much information was out there that is unknown to so many people, including me! Thank you, Jane, for your insights and advice. I really look forward to putting in place the steps you provided over the next little while."
– Beren Harris, Executive Manager for Life Strategies Expert Chris Freeman

"Before attending one of Jane's workshops, I had a healthy disdain for managing anything related to LinkedIn (even though it's critical to my consulting business). Since LinkedIn has officially recognised Jane as one of Australia and New Zealand's Top-12 LinkedIn Influencers, I figured she could teach me a thing or two. I love creating content and attracting people to my work. I loathe figuring out the technicalities of social platforms and bombarding people's inboxes with unsolicited requests. So, other than the weekly blog post, my LinkedIn strategy was avoidance. Tolerance on my best of days. In a short 45-minute seminar, Jane shifted all of that. She took me from resistance to enthusiasm, FAST. She made it easy with two insanely simple frameworks. Now I know:

1. Exactly how often to post.
2. What types of posts build credibility.
3. What types of posts build my personal brand.
4. How to do it in a way that creates little to no extra work on my part.
5. How to do it without needing to learn the technical guts of the social media platform.

Finally, it's imperative to point out how generous Jane is with her wisdom. Her desire to serve her audience is genuine and potent. Each of us left saying some version of, 'Wow, that was amazing and she is AWESOME.'"
– Dominique Quartuccio, Life By Design Expert

"Jane Anderson is the master of creating valuable connections in a modern world. She understands the key strategies that drive mutual beneficial outcomes through powerful connections like no one else. A pleasant, engaging, talented presenter with a wealth of knowledge and experience that you just cannot ignore."
– Rowdy McLean, Play a Bigger Game Expert and Motivational Speaker

"With implementation of Jane's advice, my LinkedIn profile views have increased by 275%, actions taken are up 1625%, and I have 33 new connections IN ONE WEEK! Spending no longer than five minutes a morning on this. It works, and the meetings I have been to with leads have been more productive because they have checked my profile and researched me before I arrive. An hour listening to Jane and her wealth of expertise leads me to just want to hear more. An engaging and logical presenter who absolutely knows her stuff. Go listen. Do Jane's training courses. The advice simply works."
– Maree McPherson, Diversity and Women in Leadership Expert

"Jane's knowledge and in-depth understanding of how best to leverage LinkedIn for lead generation and business growth is phenomenal. The tips and tools she shared so magnanimously in her engaging presentation enabled everyone in the room to improve how they connect on LinkedIn. I have already seen the results of implementing her advice! And if that's not enough, her warmth, approachability and generosity are truly inspiring."
– Bianka Barett, Executive Manager for Dr Jason Fox, Australian Speaker of the Year 2016

"Jane's presentation was not just full of extraordinarily useful information, it was delivered with respect, compassion and a sense of humour. Thanks so much, Jane."
– Jenny Bailey, Leadership Expert

"Jane's depth of knowledge around how to create impact using LinkedIn is unsurpassed. She walks her talk and I would recommend Jane if you need to learn how to boost your business impact using easy-to-implement steps but also gain deeper understanding of profile development and the important back-end functions of LinkedIn."
– Lisa Renn, Motivation Expert

"The depth of Jane's knowledge and experience on personal branding is ultra impressive. In particular, as a specialist in how to have IMPACT and how to CONNECT to build your practice or business, I couldn't recommend her more highly. The information she covered in a presentation I attended this week is already building my business."
– Paul Broadfoot, Innovation Expert

"Jane is a powerhouse of knowledge and an expert in maximising LinkedIn strategy, social selling on LinkedIn and B2B LinkedIn lead generation. She is incredibly generous with her knowledge, as demonstrated at a recent thought leader event where she was a keynote speaker. She was insightful, shared her expertise generously and entertaining. Jane, thank you for all the incredibly valuable tips and the effortless way you shared the immense knowledge you have so we could walk away with so many tangible actions to implement."
- **Pollyanna Lenkic, Women in Leadership Expert**

"This lady is all class and total depth. Jane knows EVERYTHING about brand and positioning. I had the privilege of seeing her present and was impressed with the thoroughness of her research and effectiveness of her strategy. Not only that, but her humility, sense of service and generous energy are inspiring. Get in line – I'm hiring her first!"
- **Zoe Routh, Leadership Expert**

"A big shout out to Jane Anderson, who presented a terrific talk on making better connections through LinkedIn at the Toowoomba Queensland Community evening at TAFE tonight. I particularly got a lot from the client quadrant you explained so well! Thanks, Jane – a lot of positive comments from all in attendance."
- **Darren Belisner, Real Estate Agent, Toowoomba**

"The value of my name and reputation has been passed down through generations in my family. Your personal brand and personalised experiences are what people really want to connect with, so much more than products. Jane's book captures some of the most practical ways to make this come to life and grow your career and business. If you get the opportunity to work with Jane, either in a one-on-one or at one of her many seminars, please do. She has certainly changed the way I look at branding my business and has helped me enormously over the past 10 years with ideas to help increase sales and improve my branding. Jane has made me realise that I have worked very hard over the past 24 years to get my name out there, and to have it respected in my industry, so therefore I should be proud to put it out there, not hide it away. She is a true professional and one of the most honest, reliable and passionate women in her industry."
- **Tracey Mathers, Leadership and Success Expert, Footwear Retailer**

"Jane presented at our recent seminar on personal branding at Griffith University, Nathan campus. It was not only insightful, it was empowering and energising. She has a very engaging aura about her and it was the most beneficial seminar I have been to as a professional. Thank you, Jane!"
- **Jessica So, Student Learning Adviser, Griffith University**

"We have had a few different workshops since doing the training and presenters have been FANTASTIC. What I'm loving is how confident the presenters are, and how they introduce themselves and engage with the audience on a personal basis. I just wanted to thank you for the training and the time you took to put the rock-star in my presenters!"
- **Casey Martone, Assistant Director, Strategic Communications IP Australia**

"Jane Anderson worked with me on my LinkedIn profile and my brand presence. Jane's professional advice was insightful and helped me to make some great positive decisions about the alignment between my image and the value I provide. The work on my LinkedIn profile paid off immediately with a new client meeting based on the First Four Seconds (one of Jane's mantras) of reading my LinkedIn profile. This meeting has led to a long-term client relationship. Jane is a clever, articulate and authentic thought leader in the space of corporate image and presence and wonderful to work with."
- **Tracey Ezard, Professional Triber, Collaborating Teams Expert**

"Jane has a thorough understanding of the career market and key drivers that matter most to employers and employees. Her greatest skill is in aligning the two and ensuring the best fit and a satisfactory outcome for both parties. In creating this area of expertise, she has engaged with people at every level and across every viewpoint. Hers is a full 360-degree understanding of what is needed and how to deliver it."
- **Flavia Formica, Leadership and Engagement Expert**

"Jane is very intelligent, dedicated and one of the most sincere individuals with whom I have had the pleasure to know. After being mentored by Jane over a 12-month period, I have seen first-hand her understanding, attention to detail and compassion for her mentees. Jane is constantly enthusiastic and extremely generous with her time. She has demonstrated through her work that she is determined to maximise results for everyone she works with through understanding their goals and what they wish to achieve. Jane is an excellent educator and teacher who instructs with inspiration and passion that can only come from the heart."
- **Ritchie Gibson, Leadership Expert and motivational Speaker**

"The Reinvent Your Career Expos are the pinnacle for career communication with adults. Jane has become an ongoing part of our events nationally to deliver key messages that offer people valuable information that ultimately changes their lives for the better. Jane is at ease with truly being able to assist people find their career passion. She speaks with such enthusiasm and credibility that she is always unable to escape after her talks. People flock towards her, hoping to gain her attention and to make arrangements to engage further with her."
- **Nicolas Riccuti, Reinvent Your Career Expo**

"I have had several dealings with Jane on behalf of some of my clients (and will continue to recommend and use her services). Her deep insight into the recruitment process was extremely valuable, particularly in the interview stages of the hiring process. In terms of career coaching, I haven't met anyone who has the understanding of the recruitment process like Jane does. At the heart of her work is a desire to make sure that the right team member lands with the right company. To me, this speaks volumes about her intentions, integrity and credibility."
– Eric Gregory, Business Coach

"Jane! I'm 'working the wheel' of social as you explained and my numbers of followed subscribers and views are going through the roof! LinkedIn views were up 533% in just a few days – whoa! They then went up to 600%. Wow! Biggest change – 'on the run' and new photos! Stepping into my true self – scary and exciting! Thanks again xxx."
– Rachel Sparks, Career Management Expert

"Jane is warm, friendly, personable, kind and she knows what she is talking about. I first met with her in what was a tough time. Speaking with her gave me my confidence back and gave me very real tools to take control of my career in moving forward. Her guidance, support and incredible knowledge in the field have provided much positive change in both my career and life. The skills that she equipped me with in moving forward have been of huge value. I originally went to her thinking it would be a once-off appointment. Now, she is an integral part of my career planning and someone I will continue to go to in the future to help me achieve my goals.
– Mish Bates, Founder, Bango PR

"Jane's insight and expertise into how to create effective SEO, content management and how to connect with people properly was just excellent and valuable. I especially loved how Jane showed us how we can manage all this in just seven minutes a day! One of the other best parts I got very excited about was the way Jane showed us how to create awesome articles. Priceless."
– Melinda Hird, Photographer

For Mark.

ABOUT THE AUTHOR

Jane Anderson is obsessed with helping experts, solopreneurs, leaders and job-seekers grow their businesses and careers, becoming more than they ever thought possible.

She is the founder of the Personal Branding Institute, an online educational organisation and directory of personal branding practitioners designed to help people become more fully self-expressed to achieve their personal and career goals.

Having helped more than 20,000 people, she has been featured on Sky Business, *The Today Show, The Age, Sydney Morning Herald*, BBC, Channel 9 and *Management Today*.

Jane holds one of the top 1% viewed LinkedIn profiles globally and is the host of the #1 ranked "Jane Anderson Brand You Show" Podcast in iTunes. She was nominated for the Telstra Business Women Awards in 2014 and 2016.

The author of four books, she is one of 12 LinkedIn Influencers in Australia and NZ and her blog has been voted #22 in the best branding blogs globally by Feedspot. She is also the creator of the Lead Generation Indicator, the world's first diagnostic for experts to identify marketing gaps in their practice.

On faculty in Thought Leaders Business School, she mentors experts to create a practice generating $500k to $1.5 million with 1-2 staff. She is also a mentor of the Queensland Government's Advancing Women in Business program. Jane speaks at conferences globally, and runs workshops and mentoring programs for organisations and the public.

Some of her clients include The International Rice Research Institute, Wesfarmers, Virgin Australia, IKEA, LEGO, Mercedes-Benz, La Trobe Institute of Molecular Science, Australian Medical Association, Shell Energy, Deakin University and Griffith University.

ACKNOWLEDGEMENTS

The key concept behind this book was one of the first pieces of work I wrote on a piece of paper in Matt Church's Thought Leaders Business School. After some colleagues looked at it with me, the feedback I received was that people didn't understand it. So, I put it away and moved on.

The good news was that I kept it, and the more I had conversations about it, the more I was able to refine it into what is now this book, the diagnostic, a workshop, a mentoring program and an online course.

So it goes without saying, thank you to Matt Church, Peter Cook, Gabrielle Dolan and Janine Garner for their guidance through this Influencer world. I'm so grateful for your encouragement, feedback and insights.

To the masters of their craft and my second family – Rowdy McLean, Keith Abraham, Nikki Fogden-Moore and Sarah Cordiner, who have had such an impact on every idea in this book and pushed me far beyond what I could have achieved on my own. This would not have happened without you.

To the clients I see every day and who work on every aspect of this book in their practices, you are such an inspiration with the ripple effect you create in the world. I am grateful to see the work behind the scenes and the constant grappling with your ideas, messaging and positioning that makes such a difference on the planet.

To the team closest to me who makes projects like this come to life. My partner, Mark, who is one of the smartest and kindest human beings on the planet. His support, along with my family, has been unconditional. The late-night proofreading and listening to the ideas in this book have been beyond invaluable. Thank you for your patience and making this come to life.

To my support team in the office, Virginia and Rhia, who share the vision to create change, educate, innovate and help people grow their practices to help others have a greater impact in the world. Thank you for your hard work and looking after everything else so I can get books like this completed!

Finally, to the editing and publishing team, Lauren Shay at Full Stop Writing, Editing and Design, and Sylvie Blair at BookPOD. Thank you for your commitment and dedication and being part of the team for every book project to date. Without you, these ideas wouldn't see the light of day.

CONTENTS

ABOUT THE AUTHOR 1

ACKNOWLEDGEMENTS 2

INTRODUCTION 5

CHAPTER 1: Why Does Being an Influencer Matter? 7

CHAPTER 2: Business Growth for Influencers 23

CHAPTER 3: Leadership 29

CHAPTER 3.1: Self-Leadership 37

CHAPTER 3.2: Thought Leadership 45

CHAPTER 3.3: Practice Leadership 53

CHAPTER 3.4: Industry Leadership 61

CHAPTER 4: Leverage 67

CHAPTER 4.1: Time 73

CHAPTER 4.2: Content 85

CHAPTER 4.3: People 93

CHAPTER 5: Lead Generation 99

CHAPTER 5.1: Direct Contact 113

CHAPTER 5.2: Network or Search 129

CHAPTER 5.3: Awareness 145

CHAPTER 5.4: Educate 171

FROM HERE 191

WANT MORE? 195

INTRODUCTION

I remember the day like it was yesterday. It was 2009 and I was at the point where I had spent nearly $30,000 of my savings on Google AdWords and search engine optimisation. I was 12 months into my coaching businesses and not getting any results. In fact, I was going backwards. I'd been working with a so-called "expert" – someone who I really trusted. Someone who I thought knew what they were doing.

When we met, this person came across as a bit of a know-all. But I believed they were trying to help me. I naively trusted this person, thinking, "Well, they're in business – they must be able to be able to help me."

This was far from reality. Things deteriorated very quickly.

I had no money left. I was trying to work out a way I could stay in business. I didn't want to go back to a job. I had done a marketing degree almost 20 years prior; however, internet marketing skills weren't taught in universities back then. In fact, I remember the day the internet was installed at my university! That's how long ago that was. Since then, the impact of the internet on growing businesses has been extraordinary.

With no money, I needed to work out exactly how I was going to grow my business. So I started with LinkedIn. LinkedIn was an online networking tool I understood, as I'd been using it in my coaching business to help people get their next job. I realised that the skills I had learnt through LinkedIn could help me grow my business and access potential buyers in the corporate world.

Through LinkedIn, I gradually rebuilt. I tried and tested as many free online tools as I could. I began to realise that there was so much potential for emerging businesses in this new digital world. Social media, newsletters, e-communications – none of these things cost money, yet they were so powerful.

Today, I work with people who are experts in their fields; whether they're just stepping out of the corporate world and getting started on their own, or seasoned entrepreneurs who need new and innovative ways to remain relevant to their markets.

I'm so excited to share this book and my diagnostic, the Lead Generation Indicator, with you. If you have a burning desire to share your expertise with the world, this book is for you.

INTRODUCTION

The reality is that by 2020, 50% of the workforce will be self-employed. It's imperative that you stand out and make an impact. This book is not only for those who want to become Influencers and leading industry experts, it's also for freelancers, solopreneurs and those who want to learn the skills that will give them cut-through in their communications and achieve business growth.

Work through the book. Make sure you watch the videos. And, of course, remember to undertake the Lead Generation Indicator questionnaire. You will be given a report that aligns with this book and identifies your specific marketing gaps. By understanding what you need to do to improve your lead-generation activity, you can grow your business, share your expertise with the world, do the work you love and get paid what you're worth.

Let's get started!

CHAPTER 1

Why Does Being an Influencer Matter?

"Marketing is like sex. Everyone thinks they're good at it."
- Steve Tobak

We are in a golden age of solopreneurs: independent, innovative experts who are turning the traditional working model on its head. No longer content with working under layers of organisational management, workers around the globe are increasingly making the decision to take full control of their careers. To carve their own niche and capitalise on their skills. To join the solo revolution.

And you are one of them. A revolutionary!

Creating your own brand has never been easier. With the explosion of social media, solopreneurs have immediate access to billions of people around the world. You can speak directly to anyone, anywhere, at any time. Likewise, the number of services and products consumers have instant access to is almost infinite. Neither business nor buyer is bound by location anymore.

It is an incredibly liberating age. But it's also one that some entrepreneurs and businesses find overwhelming.

WE'RE LIVING IN A DIGITAL-FIRST WORLD

In his book *Ctrl Alt Delete*, Mitch Joel discusses the term "digital first". He reveals the five key movements that organisations must embrace to future-proof themselves – or go out of business. One of these shifts is the fact that now, the first place your brand and business are validated is online.

Essentially, the internet and social media have the power to make or break your chances of success.

Serial entrepreneur Gary Vaynerchuk is a great example of how to cultivate a successful business by leveraging digital media. Born in the Soviet Union in 1975, Vaynerchuk immigrated to the United States in 1978. From humble beginnings, his father went on to own a liquor store in New Jersey. In the early days of the digital-first world, Vaynerchuk could see the burning potential of his father's business. After graduating from college, Vaynerchuk transformed the liquor shop into a retail wine store, which he named the Wine Library. In

2006, he started a daily video blog, *Wine Library TV*. This hugely popular webcast turned him into an internet celebrity. It attracted 90,000 viewers a day and led to a flurry of TV and speaking engagements. In just six years, Vaynerchuk grew the family business from $1 million a year to a whopping $50 million a year!

Not too bad for a small family business, right?

So, as you can see, traditional marketing has been blown out of the water. We're no longer restricted to cold calling and setting up meeting after meeting to generate leads and sales. Digital marketing has opened an array of cost-effective avenues for self-promotion and lead generation. Sales are now about leveraging your social networks, engaging with people online and educating.

This is, essentially, the social sales model:

PAST	PRESENT	FUTURE
Employees	Role Models	Ambassadors
Cold Calls	Tribes	Engagement
Sales Demonstrations	Education	Thought Leadership
Salesperson	Trusted Adviser	Expert
Transaction	Solution Selling	Lifetime Partnership

Today, the businesses and entrepreneurs that make the most impact on their audiences are role models. They're trusted advisers who create tribes – powerful online communities that help their brands grow. They educate and provide solutions. They've jumped on board the social sales train and have embraced the connection economy whole-heartedly. Because if you don't embrace change, you get left behind.

But we can't rest on our laurels. We must build on this massive sales reform and look to the future. We must become industry ambassadors; thought leaders who engage meaningfully with our followers, share generously of our expertise and regard our audiences not just as leads or dollar signs, but as lifetime partnerships.

WHY YOU NEED TO STAND OUT FROM THE CROWD

Solopreneurs are the way of the future. They account for 61% of Australian businesses.[1] And with the advent of freelance sites such as Upwork, 99designs,

---

[1] Australian Bureau of Statistics, June 2014.

Freelancer and Airtasker, an increasing number of Australians are freelancing. According to freelance marketplace Elance-oDesk, 30% of the Australian workforce – or 3.7 million people – undertake some form of freelance work.[2]

Digital marketing presents an enormous opportunity for solopreneurs. According to Ipsos Open Thinking Exchange, the average person spends two hours a day on the internet. Furthermore, IBM's Global CEO Study found that CEOs believe social media utilisation for customer engagement will increase by 256% over five years. This means social media will become the second-most popular way to engage customers after face-to-face communication.

Social media has created a level playing field. It's cheap and readily available. You don't need large amounts of money to build a solo business. You don't even need an existing client base – you can start one from scratch online. The internet has given *everyone* the potential to create a successful solo business.

But there's a downside to this equal opportunity. Despite the accessibility of social media, one of the biggest challenges entrepreneurs continue to face is finding leads and retaining clients.

The digital marketplace means you're competing against everyone else with a business like yours. You can't simply create a LinkedIn or Facebook account and expect clients to come to you. How will they know you're there? What makes you stand out? When everyone else is pushing their own unique selling point, what will make people choose *you*?

In a world where customers have immediate access to information on every kind of business around the world, it's hard to cut through the noise. To gain that competitive edge, you must create a connection.

Being a solopreneur is not enough. You must bond with your audience by offering more than your products and services alone. You need to educate, lead and gain trust. You need to make a real difference to the lives of your clients.

POSITION, POSITION, POSITION

Positioning is fundamental to creating trust and having influence. It's more than just creating an image. It's about owning your space in your industry. It's about flexing your expertise, starting conversations, changing the game, creating engaging content and enlightening others. It's about being the go-to expert for peers and clients needing guidance.

And it's what leads to sales.

---

[2] Elance-oDesk survey, 2015.

CHAPTER 1

When you have rock-solid positioning, your return on investment is second to none. Digital media and technology company Burst Media's 2014 Influencer Marketing Benchmarks Report found that on average, marketers who implemented an Influencer marketing program in 2014 received **$6.85** in earned media value for every $1 of paid media.[3] The primary tools used in Influencer marketing were:

- Blog posts
- Social syndication and branded content distribution
- Influencers and influential content

Blogs. Content. Social media. These are indispensable, cost-effective tools if you want to elevate your positioning from business owner to leading industry expert. And they are the tools that will build your audience's trust in you.

---

[3] "Report: Influencer Marketing Can Yield Big Returns." *Social Times*, March 6, 2015. http://www.adweek.com/socialtimes/report-influencer-marketing-can-yield-big-returns/616512

> *If people like you, they'll listen to you, but if they trust you, they'll do business with you.*
>
> **ZIG ZIGLAR**

CHAPTER 1

THE 12 PILLARS OF TRUST

Positioning and trust go hand in hand, and they are crucial to becoming an Influencer. In an era where our relationships with clients are increasingly conducted online, building trust is a challenge. How can you position yourself as someone your audience can depend on?

You need to consider two things:

1. How people make decisions.
2. Where to focus your attention.

Swiss psychiatrist Carl Jung identified that people make decisions based on one of two main drivers: rationale, results or outcome; and feelings, emotions or values. To build trust, you need to appeal to the "thinker" and the "feeler". You need to provide practical solutions *and* you need to connect with your audience's emotions.

So, in your communications, there should be a balance of attention: between **rational decisions** and **emotional decisions**; and between **your audience** and **yourself**. This is achieved by focusing on your audience's **problems** and solving their issues **proficiently**; and demonstrating your expert **positioning** and revealing your **personality**.

This is illustrated in the 12 Pillars of Trust model:

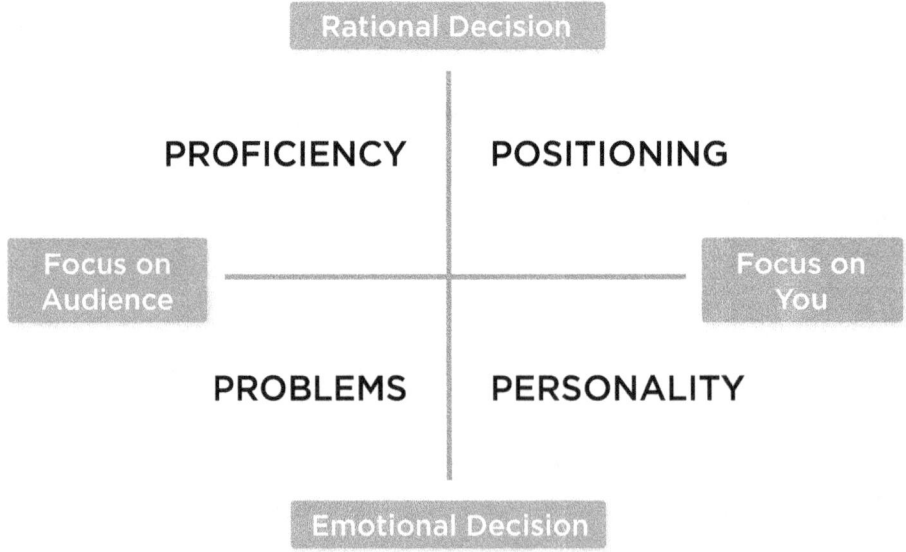

The 12 Pillars of Trust is a guide that will help you build your clients' trust. You can use it as a tool to evaluate just how trustworthy you are. Before someone decides to work with you, they will consciously and subconsciously ask themselves questions about your abilities and your character. Your job is to make it easy for them to answer these questions. This helps progress the relationship and turn the lead into a sale.

Each quadrant in the 12 Pillars of Trust consists of three activities. These will help you give your potential clients the answers they need to gain their confidence:

POSITIONING

1. **Clarity.** Be clear about who you help and what you help them with. Is it obvious who your ideal client is? Do you clearly articulate your business message?

2. **Visibility.** You need to make it easy for others to see you – in the digital marketplace and in the real world. Are you visible in the places your audience hangs out? Do you actively reach out to people who need your help?

3. **Monetary.** The price you place on your services helps others understand the value you offer. What is the value of your offering? Do your prices signify economy, business class or first class?

PROFICIENCY

1. **Mastery.** Potential clients need to know how competent you are, particularly if the issue they need resolving is complex. Do you show others how you get real results? Do you articulate the sequence of what needs to be done? Are you honest about your own past mistakes and the obstacles you've faced? Do you demonstrate how you overcame these things to become the expert you are today? What collateral do you have that shows your mastery above others (ideally, a book)?

2. **Credibility.** Your social proof is important to your buyer. What do others say about you in testimonials? Are you featured in places others can trust, such as magazines and newspapers, or at events as a speaker? Are the people who recommend you respectable? Do you have evidence that shows you deliver what you claim to deliver?

3. **Consistency.** Mixed messages disrupt the trust process. Your message needs to be consistent and delivered consistently. Is your message coherent and dependable? Do you regularly contact your potential clients

to demonstrate your expertise and ability to solve issues? Is your message clear in all you say and do – in the titles of your blogs, in your articles, videos, whitepapers and books?

PROBLEMS

1. **Validity.** When potential clients are finding more information about you, does what you say match what they are looking for? Do your collaterals – your blog posts, keynotes, webcasts, books – articulate their problems?

2. **Relevance.** What you offer must be relevant, and others must be able to relate to you. Can you demonstrate to your audience that you understand their world? Do you relate to the issues they face, their aspirations and their needs? How easy is it for others to see part of themselves in you? Are you easy to get to know?

3. **Controllability.** When something goes wrong, you need to take charge. Do you communicate and resolve issues? Or do you ignore them and let them fester? Equally as important, can you read the writing on the wall and remove yourself from situations with clients or peers that do not serve you?

PERSONALITY

1. **Remarkability.** Emphasising your unique qualities helps keep you front of mind. What makes you unique? How does your uniqueness connect with your audience's issues, values and personalities?

2. **Vulnerability.** Be honest about your vulnerabilities. What are they? Revealing your weaknesses shows that you are a real thinking, feeling person – not just an empty brand. As *Extreme Trust* authors Don Peppers and Martha Rogers say: "What is our reaction when someone presents an image of great strength and complete control, with no weaknesses? We don't trust them ... If someone only presents strengths and accomplishments, we know they are not sharing with us the full picture. If they don't trust us enough to share their weaknesses and vulnerabilities, why would we ever trust them?"

3. **Empathy.** It's essential you remain non-judgmental in your communications. You don't want to ostracise your audience or appear disinterested. Show that you genuinely care. Do you make it easy for others to be open and share their problems with you? Are you sincere? Do you keep client information confidential?

No one is perfect. You may find you do exceptionally well in one area of the 12 Pillars of Trust, but not in others. Keeping this model in mind is a great way to start building your positioning as an Influencer. It will help you nurture people's trust in you and your branding, giving you greater cut-through with your message.

Here are some questions for you to consider:

1. How do you currently share the 12 Pillars of Trust in your marketing?
2. Which pillars stand out as your strongest features?
3. If your ideal customer saw you now, what would they say stands out the most?
4. Which pillars do you need to amplify to "wow" your ideal customer?

WHY SMALL PLAYERS BUILD GREATER TRUST THAN BIG BUSINESSES

Creating trust used to be about having an office in a capital city's central business district. Now, it's about your social following, your connections and your influence. Nothing creates greater trust than content, social proof and followers.

In other words, the biggest players aren't necessarily the most powerful.

Recently, I received a call from a large organisation – a top global player in a niched sector in the IT industry. The organisation wanted to elevate its positioning, but its lead times for large sales were excessively long and inefficient. The organisation wanted to make more of an impact, more quickly.

I immediately identified that its global marketing strategy wasn't working. Because it was entirely focused on the "big organisation", the business was failing to make meaningful connections with its customers. To build trust, it needed to change tack and put its skilled team members front and centre. LinkedIn was the perfect opportunity to achieve this. I helped build LinkedIn profiles for all the team members, showcasing their insights, expertise and experience. This quickly led to increased visibility and followers for the organisation, which meant it had greater influence over its audience.

Better yet, this effective strategy was millions of dollars cheaper than its previous marketing strategy.

Patrick Hollingsworth – mountaineer, Mount Everest climber and author of *The Light and Fast Organisation* – says the successful businesses of today adopt an "alpine-style" approach to business. They are agile, use less energy and resources, and are self-reliant. Small organisations and individuals tend to have the upper hand here. They don't need large amounts of money to succeed. By their very nature, they are well equipped for navigating the constantly changing business landscape. This is in stark contrast with large organisations, which tend to have an "expedition style" of approach – a slow strategy that uses lots of time, energy and resources, and relies on a generalist skill set.

The alpine style of business embraces the digital economy. It leverages online networks and social media. It knows how to adapt to the changing needs of its markets. And it has created a formidable foe for large organisations and corporations: The Influencer.

THE ROLE OF AUTHENTICITY

Big organisations can have their glossy brochures. The small players know that the more "real" they can be with their audiences, the better.

To be real, you need to be authentic. You must demonstrate that you are genuine, dependable and trustworthy. The online world presents so many opportunities for you to express your authenticity: Snapchat, Instagram's Stories, Facebook's live video feature – just to name a few. We will investigate these further in this book.

When you are authentic in everything you say and do, you naturally create connections and build a following. This is fundamental to becoming an Influencer. As research professor and public speaker Brene Brown said, "If you think dealing with issues like worthiness and authenticity and vulnerability are not worthwhile because there are more pressing issues, like the bottom line or attendance or standardised test scores, you are sadly, sadly mistaken. It underpins everything."

So, to become an Influencer, you need to know where you are positioned *now*. Look at the following table. Where do you rate on the industry Influencer scale?

AN INDUSTRY INFLUENCER

	TYPE	POSITIONING	OBSTACLE	FOCUS	RESULT	LEADS %
5	INFLUENCER	THOUGHT LEADER	SUPPORT	LEVERAGE	TRUST	100%
4	INSTRUCTOR	EXPERT	PRODUCTIVITY	UNIQUENESS	DIFFERENTIATED	75%
3	INSIDE SECRET	HIDDEN	CONFIDENCE	AMPLIFICATION	VISIBILITY	25%
2	INCONSISTENT	CONFUSED	CLARITY	MESSAGE	IMPACT	0%
1	INVISIBLE	JUDGED	LOST	SYSTEM	PROGRESS	-10%

INVISIBLE

At this level, you're feeling a little lost with your brand and your message. You're not sure what to do and don't have the time. You could be paralysed with the fear that you'll do it all the wrong way. But while you're busy feeling lost, your audience is already making judgments about you.

You may be thinking, "How can they? They haven't even see me yet!" That's precisely the point.

If you reach out sporadically, your market will respond in a way that's based on their own preconceived ideas. You need to flip the conversation in your favour by providing your market with more information – much more information than you may realise. This will engage them and prevent them from misjudging you.

If you don't know where to start, get moving by creating an action plan. Be as specific as possible with the actions you need to take to get from A to B. Use this book as your guide. It may seem scary at first, but having a system or plan in place will soon be a source of comfort: the best thing is knowing you're starting to make progress.

INCONSISTENT

You are starting to become visible to your audience, but you aren't consistent yet. This means that you're not working as efficiently as you could be and your message lacks cut through.

From your audience's perspective, you're sharing some great content. They're

CHAPTER 1

liking and commenting on what you post, which means they want you to keep sharing. The problem is, they don't always understand what you're trying to sell, which makes it hard for you to get sales. As Australian sales expert Rachel Bourke says, "A confused mind says no."

This can be extremely frustrating. You know you're not achieving the commercial success you're capable of. The main reason you're not seeing the results is because you're not delivering your content in a way that amplifies your audience's problems. You may even be focusing on problems that aren't relevant to them. The secret here is to get crystal clear about your message. Know exactly who your market is and how you will deliver it to them. Then it's game on!

INSIDE SECRET

You may think you're easy to connect with, but you're not. At this level, you're hidden from your audience and difficult to access. This situation arises because you're worried about scaring your audience away. You end up sharing too little content across too few platforms. A lack of knowledge might also be holding you back from using different social media platforms. If that's the case, you may need help from someone you trust.

To lift your performance, you need to shift your mindset. The aim is to amplify your message across various platforms. You'll become more visible at more touch points, and in turn build greater trust with your market.

Remember, there is someone out there trying to buy you. You just have to make it easy for them.

INSTRUCTOR

You've really put in some work! It takes a lot of effort and determination to get to this point. The great news is, the most difficult work is behind you and your focus now should be on how you can show the world what you do *differently*.

At this stage, you know you have something your audience understands and wants to buy. You know how to deliver your message, address people's problems and connect with them. Now, it's time to hone in on the little things that set you apart from your competition. This comes down to your message, your personality and the markets you work with.

Writing your own book is an ideal way to make this happen. A book will amplify your message and cement your credibility. It is an essential tool that will help you move from simply being "someone who knows something" to "someone who is known for knowing something". The challenge is making time to write. You're busy, and writing a book can't be done overnight. But you need to make the effort. If you haven't got started on your book yet, now is the time!

INFLUENCER

Congratulations! You're well known in your industry. You might even say you're a thought-leader celebrity! This is because when people are asked if they've heard of you, they almost always say yes.

You've worked diligently to ensure your expertise is unique. There's a clear market for what you offer. Through consistent messaging, you've achieved the "trust nirvana" with your audience. Now, your job is to maintain that sacred space. You can do this in two ways. Firstly, look at products or programs you could use to leverage your thought leadership. These might include product offerings or licensed products you can sell to create "passive" income. You could also try to access new markets, in which case your positioning and branding will be vital. After all, you only get one chance at making a first impression!

Secondly, you need to find the right support team. At this point, it would be unusual for you not to be incredibly busy. You need some help! If you've only ever worked with a virtual team, it might be time to find an assistant locally. Your practice is now at the point where you can consider hiring an executive assistant or business manager, who can shoulder the responsibility of identifying and helping you win new work.

CHAPTER 1

> ### WANT TO FIND OUT YOUR INFLUENCER LEVEL? GO TO:
>
> https://janeandersonspeaks.com/lead-generation-indicator/
>
> *Take the free Lead Generation Indicator, valued at $80.*

QUESTIONS FOR YOU TO CONSIDER:

1. Who is the current industry Influencer in your industry?

___

2. Google their name. What do you notice they're doing?

___

3. What aspects of their trust-building and Influencer activity stand out to you?

___

4. What do you agree with?

___

5. What do you not agree with?

6. What makes you different to them?

7. Undertake the Lead Generation Indicator questionnaire. What level are you at?

8. What aspects of your report resonate with you?

9. Which aspects do you need to act on?

10. How much would you like to sell each year? What is your target?

CHAPTER 1

11. What is the average value of each lead you currently receive?

_____
_____
_____
_____

12. How many of those leads do you need to sell to achieve your target?

_____
_____
_____
_____

13. What holds you back from achieving your sales targets?

_____
_____
_____
_____

14. What needs to change so these things do not hinder your growth?

_____
_____
_____
_____

CHAPTER 2
Business Growth for Influencers

Do you ever feel as though you're doing all the right things, but your business isn't growing? Do you worry this means you might never be able to position yourself as an Influencer?

If so, you're not alone. I recently worked with a client – an expert in her field – who couldn't understand why her business was failing to grow. "I'm working really hard," she said. "I'm doing all the right things. I'm doing lots of course delivery, my pricing is competitive. But there aren't enough hours in the day. I don't know what I'm doing wrong."

When I work with industry experts and Influencers, the ones with a truly successful and sustainable business focus on these three interconnected areas:

1. LEADERSHIP

A leader has a strong vision: for themselves, their business and their industry. They inspire and motivate others through education and effective communication. There are three key elements to successful leadership:

- **Thought Leadership.** Unpack your thinking. As a thought leader, you need to clearly articulate your insights and unique perspective. Add to the body of work being done in your area of expertise. Start conversations. Anticipate and answer your audience's most pressing questions.

- **Practice Leadership.** You may be a leader in your field, but are you a leader within your own business practice? If you have staff, virtual assistants or support people, how are you leading them? How often do you touch base with them to ensure you're on the same wavelength? It's important you guide them and provide feedback so they can help drive your business in the right direction.

- **Industry Leadership.** To be the leader in your field, you must believe it and act like it. Make the most of every opportunity to demonstrate your industry leadership to others: keynotes, participating in industry forums, creating a LinkedIn group and writing your own book.

2. LEVERAGE

Use all available resources to your maximum advantage. How can you make the most of what you already have to boost your positioning, streamline processes and make more sales? The three elements of leverage are:

- **Prioritisation.** We often lament that we have no time. "There's only one of me. I can only do so much!" But what this usually means is that we're spending too much time on the wrong things. If you deal with all the "small stuff" first and don't prioritise your time, you'll lose focus of the big picture and miss the more profitable opportunities.

- **Your Team.** Too often, we try to spread ourselves too thin. To remain focused on your vision, you must manage and leverage your team effectively. What skills do they have? Are there any gaps in their capabilities? Delegate where possible and decide if you can work with a virtual team or whether you need support staff with you on the front line.

- **Positioning.** Once you unpack your thought leadership, use it to its absolute potential to grow your positioning. Think once and use often. This means making the most of social media, keynotes, workshops and mentoring sessions to share your expertise and drive home your key message. You then become known for knowing something.

3. LEAD GENERATION

This is fundamental to your sales pipeline. A lead-generation strategy will help you find new leads and clients. This isn't about "hustling" people. Remember, being an Influencer means genuinely wanting to help people. Successful lead generation is about educating your target market: the people who would benefit the most from your services.

- **Influence.** Don't sit back and wait for sales to magically appear. Take control over the sales process to get more clients and grow your business. People are more likely to work with someone they know, like and trust. These things are essential to having influence. So, reach out to your audience, educate them, connect with them and foster positive relationships – online and offline.

- **Income.** When you have a lead-generation strategy, your income will increase. But you also need a sales target. Know what you want to earn and create a strategy that details the exact steps you need to take to achieve that figure.

- **Indicators.** These are quantifiable measures that indicate whether what you're doing is working or not. For example, the number of new e-newsletter subscribers you receive in a month, the number of people who register for your webinar, the number of social media followers you have. These give you an idea of the amount of leads and potential sales you are creating.

The Practice Growth Model below demonstrates how the three key areas of Leadership, Leverage and Lead Generation overlap and work together to achieve **business growth**:

PRACTICE GROWTH MODEL

POSITIONING

PRACTICE — PEOPLE

Leadership
Platform
Leverage
Business Growth
Pricing   Sales
Lead Generation

INFLUENCE — INDICATORS

INCOME

At the intersection of **Leadership** and **Leverage**, you can amplify your area of expertise – through your thought leadership, use of time, your team and positioning. This is called **platform**.

At the intersection of **Leverage** and **Lead Generation**, your focus is on your system itself to increase your **sales**. By leveraging your team's skills and prioritising your time, you can focus on using your positioning to access buyers and grow your practice.

CHAPTER 2

At the intersection of **Leadership** and **Lead Generation**, you need to focus on industry leadership and innovation to drive up your **pricing**. Effectively managing your business practice means you can spend more time contributing to your industry and bringing greater results for your clients, which leads to more profitable sales.

So, if you're concerned your business isn't growing as it should, don't simply throw your hands up in the air. By focusing on Leadership, Leverage and Lead Generation, you can see what steps you need to take to make your Influencer business a profitable and sustainable one.

QUESTIONS FOR YOU TO CONSIDER:

1. If you were to be an expert in thinking, what kind of thinking would it be?

___

2. Have you led a team in your current or previous job? What worked well? What didn't work well?

___

3. Have you written articles or blogs for a newsletter or publication? If not, would you like to write some and where would you like them published?

___

4. How productive are you? Do you try to identify and establish patterns, habits and routines to improve your efficiency?

___

5. How do you leverage your team, colleagues and other people you work with? How do you avoid spreading yourself too thin?

___

6. How often do you take the initiative to contact your networks and people you know?

___

CHAPTER 2

7. Who do you catch up with and hang out with the most?

_____
_____
_____
_____

8. If you could work with your ideal target market, who would they be?

_____
_____
_____
_____

9. When was the last time you bought something of high price? What was it?

_____
_____
_____

10. When was the last time you bought something of low price? What was it?

_____
_____
_____
_____

11. What differences did you experience as a customer?

_____
_____
_____

12. Have you used key performance indicators to measure your performance in a previous job? If so, what aspects of your job were measured?

_____
_____
_____

CHAPTER 3
Leadership

"Leadership is about making others better as a result of your presence and making sure that impact lasts in your absence."
– Sheryl Sandberg

South African business magnate and inventor Elon Musk is one of the most innovative tech leaders in the world. As the founder of SpaceX and Tesla Motors, he is redefining the future of transportation in space and on Earth.

In March 2016, Musk unveiled Tesla's highly anticipated Model 3, a $35,000 electric car. This signaled an unprecedented threat to the mainstream car industry. In just one week, the Model 3 attracted a whopping 325,000 pre-orders.[1] If this wasn't enough to make the traditional automobile companies nervous, in April 2017, it was revealed that Tesla had surpassed General Motors to become the most valuable car maker in the US.[2]

Who would have thought that a global market as formidable as the auto industry could be dealt such a blow by the vision of one man?

Musk is the epitome of successful business leadership. When Musk speaks, people listen. His companies and inventions offer enormous benefit to the world; benefits he steadfastly believes in.

Leaders must not only have strong conviction and self-belief – they must also be adaptable. They must have the willingness and ability to continue to grow and push the boundaries of their business and thought leadership.

One client, Adam Voigt, is a shining example of this. Previously a school principal, Voigt elevated his positioning by becoming a leader and keynote speaker in the education sector. He became a trailblazer in his market: what is known as a "category killer". He presented a TED Talk at the inaugural TEDx Darwin event, has been featured on TV as a bullying expert, and has spoken

---

1 "We are now witnessing Elon Musk's slow-motion disruption of the global auto industry." *Quartz*, April 8, 2016, https://qz.com/656443/we-are-now-witnessing-elon-musks-slow-motion-disruption-of-the-global-auto-industry/
2 "Tesla surpasses GM to become most valuable car company in US." *The Guardian*, April 11, 2017, https://www.theguardian.com/technology/2017/apr/10/tesla-most-valuable-car-company-gm-stock-price

CHAPTER 3

at international conferences about education and school culture. At the heart of Voigt's message was the need to build meaningful, productive partnerships to succeed. Voigt saw a gap in the corporate market for this kind of thought leadership. So, he built upon his messages of learning and partnerships and took them to a whole new level. Voigt successfully grew his teams, businesses, companies and organisations to reach new levels of performance and leadership.

Leadership is fundamental to becoming an Influencer. Let's look at the four fundamental layers of successful leadership.

LAYERS OF LEADERSHIP

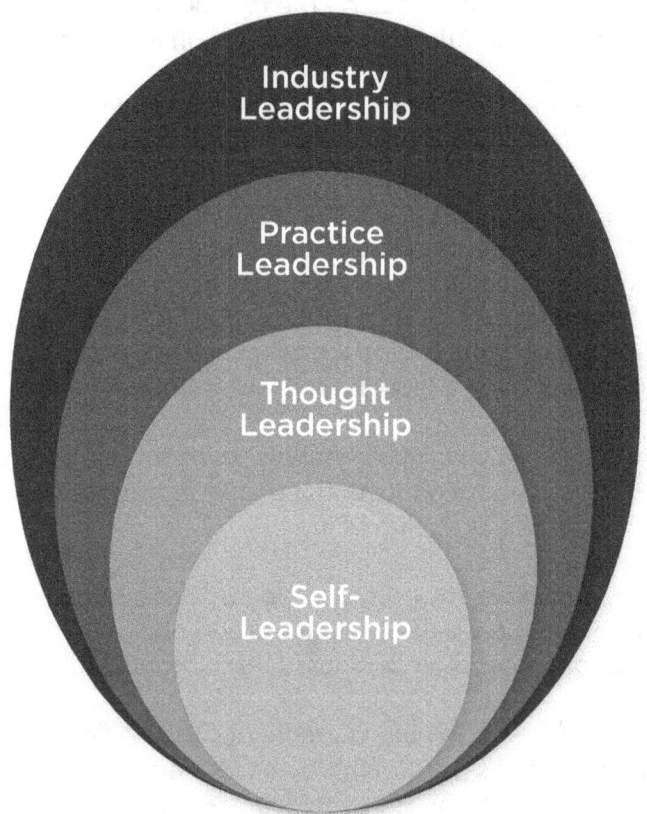

Becoming an industry Influencer is a bit like painting a piece of antique furniture. The layers of leadership start with yourself. Just like sanding and undercoating, you need the discipline and tenacity to build something of value. The next level is your thought leadership, which is akin to the first coat of paint. Once this coat has dried, the second coat is your practice leadership. The final coat is the glossy varnish that represents your industry leadership.

The easy option is to spray paint the piece of furniture. However, by building strong foundations and being thorough, you'll create an authentic platform. The layers are what give you impact so you can become a category killer with your message.

You must work hard. Being known as an expert doesn't suddenly happen and it's not a matter of luck. You must make the conscious decision to look outside yourself and identify the contribution you want to make to your industry. You must make the strategic choice to deliver at the Influencer level. It's essential you have that commitment to excellence and the belief that you can be the best in the country, or even the best in the world, at what you do.

SELF-LEADERSHIP

Self-leadership is about personal responsibility. It's the ability to take charge, be intentional and act with purpose. How do you intend to be seen, what do you want to be known for and what message do you have that can transform the lives of others? If you wait for success to happen, it won't happen. Bestsellers don't happen by mistake. World champions don't happen by mistake. They are the result of an intense clarity of goals, strategy, sequence and discipline.

THOUGHT LEADERSHIP

Thought leadership is about your area of expertise. It's the lens through which you see the world and it brings impact to your leadership. As Matt Church, the founder of Thought Leaders Business School, says: "It's the difference between knowing something versus being known for knowing something."

PRACTICE LEADERSHIP

Regardless of whether you have a virtual assistant working with you five hours per week, or a group of people helping you run your practice, you need to lead your team. Sitting back and expecting others to drive your business forward won't work. Your team needs to be inspired. Share with them your vision. Support and guide them with trust and autonomy so they can help you achieve your goals.

INDUSTRY LEADERSHIP

In his book *The Discipline of Market Leaders*, corporate strategy expert Michael Treacy likens industry leadership to a tricycle. The tricycle is comprised of three core business strategies: operational excellence, customer intimacy and product leadership. All three strategies must be present if you

CHAPTER 3

want to become an industry leader. But the direction your tricycle takes depends on the strategy your front wheel is focused on. Which strategy will give you the edge in becoming a market leader? In an expert's world, you not only need to be clear on your message, you need to make a decision about the strategy behind your message to make the most impact in your industry.

> *Leadership is not about a title or a designation. It's about impact, influence and inspiration. Impact involves getting results, influence is about spreading the passion you have for your work, and you have to inspire team-mates and customers.*
>
> — ROBIN SHARMA

CHAPTER 3

QUESTIONS FOR YOU TO CONSIDER:

1. Who do you admire as a leader? Why?

_____
_____
_____
_____

2. What traits do they have that you may have?

_____
_____
_____

3. How do you demonstrate those traits?

_____
_____
_____

4. What are you most passionate about in your life and work?

_____
_____
_____
_____

5. Who do you inspire the most?

_____
_____
_____

6. How do you know?

_____
_____
_____
_____

7. When have you taken on a leadership role within an organisation? What was the experience like?

___

8. What did you enjoy?

___

9. What didn't you enjoy?

___

10. What did you learn?

___

11. If you had your time again, what would you have done differently?

___

12. On a scale of 1 to 10, how comfortable are you about taking the lead?

___

13. On a scale of 1 to 10, how comfortable are you about making unpopular decisions?

___

CHAPTER 3

14. When have you played out front? What was the experience like?

_____
_____
_____

15. On a scale of 1 to 10, how much do you value excellence in your work?

_____
_____

16. In which aspects of your work do you obsess about excellence?

_____
_____
_____

17. When have you noticed changes in a market, a shift in customer needs or new ideas in the world? Which of those did you act upon?

_____
_____
_____

18. What was the result?

_____
_____
_____

19. When have you noticed that an organisation has needed to do something more effectively?

_____
_____
_____

20. What did you do about it?

_____
_____

CHAPTER 3.1
Self-Leadership

"For a man to conquer himself is the first and noblest of all victories."
– Plato

Gary Vaynerchuk, bestselling author and key Influencer around marketing and business growth, says self-awareness is the most powerful tool you can have in your leadership arsenal.

Self-leadership is about self-management and personal responsibility. It's like choosing to drive a manual car instead of a self-driving Tesla car. When you drive a manual car, you get back to basics. You're more aware of what you're doing. Your focus is on the gears, your speed and the twists and turns of your journey. It's the same with leadership. You cannot be on autopilot and let the world drive you. You're in control. You make the decisions.

To lead others, you must first lead yourself. You must be highly focused and disciplined. You must be in control of your circumstances. And you must have the conviction that you are an indispensable source of knowledge on your subject and topic.

So, why do some people get ahead and others don't? Why do some people stand out and others languish at the sidelines? Why is it that some people say the right things, but can't actually do the job?

I grew up in a small town called Lismore in northern New South Wales, Australia. Due to its proximity to a river, Lismore is prone to flooding, with a major flood occurring on average every seven years. Each year, the emergency services team reveals on the radio what level the river is expected to rise. They do this so business owners can prepare accordingly.

Recently, a levee bank was constructed to stop water flowing into the town when the river burst its banks. However, a once-in-a-hundred-year flood suddenly raged through the town after an incredible downpour in a short period of time. There had been no flood warning from emergency services on the radio, so many of the business owners in town did nothing and lost much of their stock. The people who had run their businesses in town for many years knew from experience not to leave anything to chance when it rained; they had already moved their stock and fittings to higher ground by the time the flood hit. They didn't need to wait around to be told!

In other words, the businesses owners with a high level of self-leadership took action early. They were proactive, taking matters into their own hands. As unfortunate it was for the businesses that did not act, failing to anticipate risks and failing to mitigate risks are not signs of self-leadership.

Psychologist Daniel Goleman, author of *Emotional Intelligence*, says exceptional leaders distinguish themselves with their superior self-leadership.

This is demonstrated by a study conducted by Green Peak Partners,[1] which assessed 72 executives in public and private companies with a turnover of $50 million to $5 billion. The study found that a higher self-awareness score was the strongest predictor of overall business success. Furthermore, the executives who were more aware of their weaknesses tended to make better decisions for the business. They were more likely to hire subordinates who could perform better on tasks outside the executives' skill sets.

Self-leadership is complex. In fact, Dr John Ng – leadership expert, researcher and author of the book *Dim Sum Leadership* – says there are four aspects of self-leadership:

1. **Self-awareness.** The ability to acknowledge and understand your values, strengths, weaknesses and emotional needs.
2. **Self-management.** The ability to nurture and harness your passions, abilities, emotions and leadership capacity in decision-making.
3. **Other-awareness.** The ability to recognise the passions, strengths, weaknesses, needs and potential of others.
4. **Other-management.** The ability to motivate others to reach their potential and fulfill the objectives of the business or organisation.

In my experience with my own practice and working with clients, I believe there are three additional aspects of self-leadership:

- **Time Management.** The ability to manage time instead of letting time manage you. This means planning your week, month and year, preparing for meetings, and ensuring your staff know how to help you get prepared.

- **Stress Management.** The ability to manage adversities, challenges and issues. The way you deal with your own stress impacts your capacity to

---

[1] "Research Results: Nice Guys Finish Last When it Comes to Company Performance." Green Peak Partners, June 15, 2010, http://www.marketwired.com/press-release/research-results-nice-guys-finish-first-when-it-comes-to-company-performance-1276170.htm

lead others. How long does it take for you to overcome challenges? What strategies do you use to create resilience?

- **Decision Making.** The ability to make decisions quickly. Do you know when the time is right to go ahead or delay? Do you procrastinate and put things off until tomorrow? It's important you know how to break down complex problems to identify the actual issues. Do you take all parties into account? How aware are you of your environment so that you can anticipate issues when making decisions?

The success of any leader greatly depends on the way they lead themselves. As Dee Hock, founder and former CEO of Visa, says, "We should invest 50% of our leadership amperage in self-leadership, and the remaining 50% should be divided into leading down, leading up and leading laterally."

CHAPTER 3.1

QUESTIONS FOR YOU TO CONSIDER:

1. In your heart of hearts, what do you believe are your strengths?

_____
_____
_____
_____

2. What are your weaknesses?

_____
_____
_____

3. What are your emotional needs from your family, partner, colleagues, team and friends?

_____
_____
_____

4. How do your emotions affect your decision making?

_____
_____
_____

5. How do your emotions affect your decision making under pressure?

_____
_____
_____

6. How well do you recognise strengths in others?

_____
_____
_____
_____

7. When have you recognised the potential in another and supported them to flourish?

_____
_____
_____
_____

8. What do you do to support others to achieve their potential?

_____
_____
_____
_____

9. How well in advance do you plan your schedule?

_____
_____
_____

10. When something goes wrong, do you take control to rectify the problem or leave it as it is?

_____
_____
_____

11. Who do you think has great self-leadership and self-motivation?

_____
_____
_____

12. How much do you think success in life is driven by luck?

_____
_____
_____
_____

CHAPTER 3.1

13. Think of a time when you faced a challenging situation. What happened? What did you do to overcome it? What did you learn?

_____
_____
_____
_____

14. What do you find yourself telling others when they go through challenging situations?

_____
_____
_____

15. What do you say to others to inspire them and give them hope during challenging times?

_____
_____
_____

16. What traits do you have that don't serve you well in your business or career?

_____
_____
_____

17. How do you manage or mitigate your natural biases?

_____
_____
_____

18. Who are your board of directors? Who do you surround yourself with daily and weekly? How will they help you move to where you want to go?

_____
_____
_____

19. How often do you ask for feedback?

_____
_____
_____
_____

20. Who do you ask for feedback? Are they qualified to give it to you?

_____
_____
_____
_____

CHAPTER 3.1

CHAPTER 3.2
Thought Leadership

"Thought leaders advance the marketplace of ideas by posting actionable, commercially relevant, research-backed, new points of view. They engage in 'blue ocean strategy' thinking on behalf of themselves and their clients, as opposed to simply churning out product-focused, brand-centric white papers or curated content that shares or mimics others' ideas."
– Craig Badings and Liz Alexander

In his bestselling book, *Blink: The Power of Thinking Without Thinking*, US journalist Malcolm Gladwell describes artists who are charged with the job of determining whether a sculpture is a fake. Those considered experts, ie. those who had more than 10,000 hours' experience examining genuine art, were able to identify the fake art in the blink of an eye. Thus, Gladwell contends that 10,000 hours is "the magic number of greatness".

In other words, establishing your thought leadership requires a huge investment in time and practice. It also means having a thorough understanding of your strengths and skills, and the ability to capitalise on them.

A great example of this is one of my clients, Michelle. Michelle was the property manager for a family that owned 18 buildings in Brisbane. Her job was to train the family's daughter to take over the business.

Michelle came to me feeling unfulfilled, as though there was no career progression for her. But she didn't know what other kind of job to look for. Looking through Michelle's resume, I noticed that most of the roles she'd had previously had started in business development or sales, then turned into training roles.

After undertaking the Myers-Briggs Type Indicator® assessment, Michelle discovered she had an ENFJ personality type – Extroverted, Intuitive, Feeling, Judging. ENFJs are natural teachers and leaders who inspire others to better themselves. Michelle had been an educator for most of her life, even though she might not have called herself that. After looking at all her achievements, her story and her expertise, it was clear that Michelle was all about giving people the chance to achieve their potential.

When I pointed this out to her, she became teary. No one had ever said that to her before. Until then, Michelle had never been clear on her true strengths, skills or passions. She realised that she had spent so many years doing what she was good at, but not what she loved. She was now free to do what she wanted to do in a different space, using her 10,000 hours – her thought leadership – for a higher purpose.

KNOW YOUR STRENGTHS AND YOUR WEAKNESSES

Thought leadership is key to becoming an Influencer. It's what you want to be known for. Remember, it's not good enough to simply know something – you want to be known for knowing something. So, if you're a little unclear on your thought leadership, you need to work out your strengths.

How can you do this? A simple way is to do an assessment of your strengths. We often find it easier to identify our weaknesses, but to move forward and take responsibility for the direction of your life and career as an Influencer, you must be able to identify both, and amplify the strengths you possess.

We all have something that sets us apart from others, so start thinking about your strengths:

- What are your advantages?
- What do you do well?
- Why did you decide to enter the field you are in?
- What motivated and influenced you?
- Are they still part of your inherent strengths?
- What need do you expect to fill within your organisation or position?
- What are your most notable achievements?
- What knowledge or expertise will you bring to your business and clients that may not have been available to them before?
- What is your greatest asset? What has led to your successes?

Ultimately, your personal brand and positioning as an Influencer begin with you. Until you know yourself better, you can't effectively convey who you are to anyone else. By singling out your strengths, passions and expertise, and being honest with yourself about your weaknesses, you will find clarity and focus. It will enable you to share your knowledge and elevate your thought leadership.

Some questions to consider as you reflect on your strengths and weaknesses:

- If you woke up tomorrow with an ideal life, what would it look like?
- How do you want to be remembered? What would the speech at your 80th birthday sound like?

- How well positioned are you to ask for what you want in your salary or fees?

Once you are clear on your strengths and the key messages of your thought leadership, you can start to position yourself with a content plan. In 2014, $135 billion was spent on content marketing.[1] It is set to become a $300 billion industry by 2019.[2] This means that organisations and customers are buying your authenticity and your brand. Those who are the most authentic are the most bought. We'll be covering content marketing in more detail later in this book.

As Steve Jobs said, "Focus and simplicity is one of my mantras. Simple can be harder than complex. You must work hard to get your thinking clean to make it simple. It's worth it in the end, because once you get there, you can move mountains."

YOUR THOUGHT LEADERSHIP MAKES YOU UNIQUE

Thought leadership is a bit like notching up the kilometers on your car. It's not necessarily the type of car you drive – in other words, the kinds of jobs you've had – that matters. It's your accumulative experience and the skills you've gradually built and consistently used that count.

If I looked at your work history, what's the common thread in all the roles you've had? Where have you been? What have you done? How do your experiences add up to create your unique thought leadership?

Thought leadership is the lens through which you see the world. The challenge is to make this lens valuable to others. How can others learn from your thought leadership? How can it benefit them so that they buy from you? Essentially, it's about clarifying your mastery. Your thought leadership must make an impact on the world and for the world of others.

In fact, thought leadership is not only desirable, but essential if you want to survive in business. By 2020, 50% of the workforce will be self-employed.[3] According to South African futurist and strategy consultant Dr Graeme Codrington, the people who know how to market and brand themselves for the future will be the ones who survive. And to do that, you must be able to

---

1 "20 Captivating Content Marketing Facts in 2014." Jeffbullas.com, http://www.jeffbullas.com/2014/07/23/0-captivating-content-marketing-facts-in-2014/#mPy71V53BSrk04KZ.99
2 "Content marketing will be a $300 billion industry by 2019." Marketing, July 10, 2015, https://www.marketingmag.com.au/news-c/content-marketing-will-300-billion-industry-2019/
3 "The Rise of the Freelancer Economy." Forbes, January 26, 2016, https://www.forbes.com/sites/brianrashid/2016/01/26/the-rise-of-the-freelancer-economy/#103efc593bdf

CHAPTER 3.2

unpack your insights and understanding. This has been identified in the Future Work Skills 2020 Report as "sense-making".

We are increasingly living in a world of knowledge workers – people whose job it is to think for a living. In Australia, four out of five people are employed in a service-based business. This isn't going to change any time soon.

So, to grow this type of business and succeed in this era of knowledge workers, you must be on top of your content. It takes 10 pieces of content before somebody decides to work with you, and 90% of that decision is made before they even get in touch with you. Sharing your thought leadership is key.

WHAT'S YOUR CATEGORY?

Shelley Barrett, CEO of cosmetics brand ModelCo, says to succeed, it's essential that you truly understand your industry. "When I went into business, I thought I was going into the world of beauty, when in actual fact I was going into the world of retailing, wholesaling, marketing, logistics, finance."[4]

One of the greatest challenges for industry experts and thought leaders is to make sure they can be easily bought. Creating a message you're passionate about is one thing. Making sure that message has a buyer and can generate an income is another. It's important to be clear on the actual problems you solve so your product can be bought easily.

Once people know how to buy you, you can differentiate yourself from the rest. But if you try to be too clever, you will repel your market. They might not even understand what they're buying from you. Know the category you're appealing to with your thought leadership so you stay on message and make the most impact.

Here are some sample categories of how expertise and branding are bought across public and private markets:

THOUGHT LEADERSHIP	CORPORATE CATEGORY	PUBLIC CATEGORY
Organisational Futurist	• Culture • Leadership • Futurist	• Leadership
Personal Branding	• Communication • Marketing • Leadership • Influence • Confidence	• Communication • Marketing • Leadership • Confidence
Lifestyle Strategist	• Productivity	• Weight Loss • Work/Life Balance
Intrigue Expert	• Storytelling • Communication • Influence	• Communication • Marketing

---

[4] "ModelCo founder Shelley Barrett shares her two best pieces of business advice." *Mamamia*, November 11, 2015.

QUESTIONS FOR YOU TO CONSIDER:

1. When you think of your "10,000 hours", what words come to mind?

___

2. What do you see as the greatest hurdles for people in their roles at work or in their lives?

___

3. What frustrates you about people or the world?

___

4. What do you think would make people happier, more engaged, more productive and more conscious?

___

5. When have you actively disagreed with something or someone?

___

6. What do you wish you'd known that you found out the hard way?

___

THOUGHT LEADERSHIP

7. What advice do you repeatedly give to others, such as your team, your manager and your family or friends?

_____
_____
_____

8. What was something that you found difficult to learn?

_____
_____

9. If you were to speak at your dream conference, what would it be? What would you speak about?

_____
_____
_____

10. What do you get referred for? What skill or task attracts people to you when they need help?

_____
_____
_____

11. If you were to sell what you know, what category would that fit into? Corporate or public?

_____
_____
_____

12. What markets could your area of expertise be sold to?

_____
_____

13. Who do you already know in those markets?

_____
_____
_____

EXPERT TO INFLUENCER

CHAPTER 3.2

14. Where do those markets congregate? Do they have industry events? How do they get together? Do they have an annual conference?

_____
_____
_____

15. Who runs those events? Can you find them on a website or on LinkedIn?

_____
_____
_____

16. What does that market value? Eg. Productivity, sales, engagement, performance, energy, looking beautiful, consciousness.

_____
_____
_____

17. Do your markets spend money on the subject?

_____
_____
_____

18. Who else is an expert on the subject?

_____
_____
_____

19. What makes you unique?

_____
_____
_____

20. What aspect of your thought leadership might be missing in your branding?

_____
_____

CHAPTER 3.3
Practice Leadership

"Be a yardstick of quality. Some people aren't used to an environment where excellence is expected."
– Steve Jobs

Practice leadership is, essentially, individual leadership. You need to create a collective of leaders around you. The people in your team must be leaders within their own roles. They must show initiative, find solutions and take charge. You don't have the time to look after people who need mothering.

I know first-hand how essential it is to have a team of leaders on my side. I recently went through a recruitment drive with my own staff. I needed an executive assistant: someone with an abundance of experience, who could take charge of the role, who didn't need a lot of direction and who could identify opportunities for the business to move it forward.

Fortunately, I found Virginia. Virginia had worked for CEOs of various companies and had demonstrated true leadership in her roles. She was exactly what I was after. As my executive assistant, Virginia is empowered to make decisions about the business. She is a true leader of her role and helps me drive the business in the direction it needs to go.

So, create an environment where your team members can work to their strengths. Nurture their desire to achieve success. Make it challenging, inspiring and rewarding so everyone on your team can be a leader. The benefits of this are mutual.

RECRUIT THE RIGHT TALENT

Recruiting the right talent can save you a lot of stress. According to *Freelance Folder*, the top stressors that keep freelancers and entrepreneurs awake at night include: deadlines, finances, finding clients, client conflicts, interruptions, administration tasks and sickness.[1] All these things can significantly impact your business, but this impact can be reduced if you have the right talent on your team.

---

[1] "How to Overcome Freelancing Stress." *Freelance Folder*, June 17, 2010, http://freelancefolder.com/overcoming-freelancing-stress/

CHAPTER 3.3

Furthermore, know what kind of contractors and suppliers you need to engage. Even though you might not hire them as employees, they are still part of your team. You need to know that they are the right people to work with. Find out as much as you can about them. Do they have testimonials? Are they highly recommended by others? Do they turn up in Google search results?

Identify the leadership skills in your contractors as you would your staff. Help them develop those skills further. This will not only help them achieve their own personal and business success; it will contribute to yours as well.

The key areas to finding leverage in your practice are:

- **Time.** Time is such a finite resource, especially if your practice is just you and a virtual assistant or executive assistant. Your time must be focused on revenue-generating activities and the least amount of administrative tasks.

    Getting support as soon as you can will help your business grow faster. One of the challenges is knowing what to delegate and what not to delegate.

    Some of the activities you might like to consider include:

    - Social media
    - Bookkeeping
    - Calendar management
    - Travel management
    - Event management
    - Customer service

    As Steve Jobs said, "It's really clear that the most precious resource we all have is time."

- **Continuous improvement.** Having a systems mindset of consistent improvement will create significant return on investment of your time. The Japanese have a word for this called "kaizen", which was created in the Toyota factory after World War II. It was used to identify ways to improve processes and reduce waste in all aspects of the business, from logistics and management to purchasing. It has since been used across a broad range of industries, including health care, government, coaching and finance.

    In my first full-time job, I worked for the Mathers family, which owned a chain of footwear stores across Australia. Sir Robert Mathers was the patriarch of the family business. One of his business mantras was to build a "brick on a brick". This meant planning and debriefing every business exercise, and looking at innovative ways to work more effectively.

To improve your systems, focus on the following areas:

- Capturing procedures and processes for all tasks and keeping them updated. This can be completed by your executive assistant.
- Planning and scheduling time to undertake your own work, as well as client-facing delivery.
- Technology that supports your business-growth activities, such as CRM (Customer Relationship Management), newsletter management, email and collaboration tools.
- Debriefing and planning programs for the future, based on customer demand and changes to the market.

As writer Mark Twain said, "Continuous improvement is better than delayed perfection."

- **Capability.** Ensure your team members have the right skills and attributes required for the job. It's easy to let someone into your team because you like them, but have they got the ability to undertake the role?

  Equally, it's just as important that you build your team based on where you want your business to go, not where you are right now. Consider the goals and aspirations you have. The right people they will take you there, rather than you having to carry them there. Team members who have initiative and personal responsibility are what you need.

- **Communication.** Ensure your lines of communication are open and fast. Weekly meetings with daily interruptions are the least productive way for teams to communicate. It will negatively impact your business growth as you focus less on customer experiences while you constantly put out fires. Streamlined communication processes mean the team can connect, gain feedback quickly, debrief and plan for the short and long term.

- **Collaboration.** The more you can get let go and allow your team to collaborate with you and between themselves, the more diversity of thought is achieved.

  As the leader of the team, and yes, this means suppliers as they're a part of your team, you need to allocate time for proactive brainstorming and decision making. If you have remote or offshore staff or supporters, ensure they still feel part of the team. Let them be heard and give them the opportunity to make a contribution, even though they may not be there in person.

CHAPTER 3.3

> *Employers and business leaders need people who can think for themselves — who can take initiative and be the solution to problems.*
>
> — **STEPHEN COVEY**

QUESTIONS FOR YOU TO CONSIDER:

1. When have you led a team in the past?

2. What do you do best as a leader?

3. How do you know when you're not effective as a leader?

4. How comfortable are you in making unpopular decisions?

5. When have you done that? What was the outcome?

6. What would you have done differently?

7. Have you terminated any staff? If so, how many and what have you learnt from the experience?

_____
_____
_____

8. Do you have a systems mindset?

_____
_____
_____

9. If not, do you know what you need to do to create a systems mindset and develop it within your team?

_____
_____
_____

10. How do you know when you've found good talent? What do you do about it when you do find them?

_____
_____
_____

11. Have you ever worked with a supplier who had no integrity in their work? What did you learn? What will you do differently next time you engage a contractor?

_____
_____
_____

12. What process currently causes the most friction in your practice? Travel? Coaching bookings? Speaking? Running workshops?

_____
_____
_____
_____

13. What's the one thing you could do differently to improve that process?

_____
_____
_____

14. How long will it take to make this change? When will you do it?

_____
_____
_____

15. Who are the contractors, suppliers and staff who take the most initiative?

_____
_____
_____

16. How can you leverage that even more? (Hint: Are there other certain tasks they like doing or other goals they want to achieve?)

_____
_____
_____
_____

17. When recruiting talent to support you, what questions have you created to identify the best candidate?

_____
_____
_____
_____

18. How will you eliminate the wrong candidates?

_____
_____
_____
_____

CHAPTER 3.3

19. What will be the impact if you choose the right person?

_____
_____
_____
_____

20. What will be the impact if you choose the wrong person?

_____
_____
_____
_____

> # CHAPTER 3.4
Industry Leadership

Tracey Hughes was born in the UK and backpacked to Australia in her teens. At 18, she took up a hairdressing apprenticeship. After proving to be a pretty good stylist, she was asked if she would attend an event to show people how she cut. Not really understanding what this meant, she agreed and was relieved she didn't have to speak – just show people how she cut hair.

What Tracey didn't know was that she would have to commentate and explain the way she was cutting. She froze, but then took a deep breath and started talking and explaining what she was doing. It seemed she had an unrealised ability to speak in public. Before she knew it, Tracey was being asked to speak to more audiences who wanted to learn her unique skill and style of cutting hair.

Today, Tracey graces the global stage. She's spoken to more than 500,000 salon professionals. With more than 20,000 Instagram followers, she has a bevy of awards to her name. These include:

- Certified Speaking Professional
- International Haircut of the Year
- 4 x Educator of the Year
- 4 x Excellence in Education
- 10 x Salon of the Year
- 2 x Hairdresser of the Year
- 2 x Creative Colourist of the Year
- Australian Masters
- People's Choice

What sets Tracey apart is something called her "value proposition". She helps her clients by speaking at events and conferences. She is totally customer focused. Whether she is talking about the participants attending her events, her in-store customers or the clients she supports, such as event planners and sponsors, Tracey is 100% committed to the customer experience. This has been Tracey's "front wheel" for her entire working career.

In their book *The Discipline of Market Leaders*, Michael Treacy and Fred Wiersema researched 80 market-leading industries and identified that there were three key drivers or wheels that an industry-leading organisation could have. These are:

- Operational Excellence
- Product Leadership
- Customer Intimacy

Treacy and Wiersema say that as an industry leader, you need to choose *one* of these drivers as your front wheel. If you try to do all three, you'll be spread too thin and not be known for knowing something.

In an expert world, this same approach works on two levels: knowing what your customer's front wheel is so you can speak the same language, and understanding what your front wheel is so you're playing to your strengths.

Industry leadership is crucial to removing commoditisation. There is no point having a name and a big price on your services if you can't prove that you're the best at what you do. Customers will pay for the level of an industry leader so long as you can provide evidence that you are the best.

It's a bit like buying a ticket for first class, business class or economy. Industry leaders are first class and business class. You lead the way for economy. You are the trendsetter!

So, you need to undertake activities to demonstrate that you are business class. Some of these activities include:

- Speaking at industry events and conferences, possibly globally.
- Undertaking PR activities, such as media interviews and writing for publications.
- Winning and/or being nominated for industry awards.
- Pricing that represents industry leadership standard.
- Being on industry committees and groups.
- Mentoring others in the industry.

These are just a few ways to help you not only stand out in a noisy world, but to shape an industry, to make an impact at a larger and deeper scale, and to deepen your message and identity in that industry.

As Steve Jobs said, "It's not about charisma and personality, it's about results and products and those very bedrock things that are why people at Apple and outside of Apple are getting more excited about the company and what Apple stands for and what its potential is to contribute to the industry."

QUESTIONS FOR YOU TO CONSIDER:

1. What industry associations are you a member of?

___

2. Have you ever spoken at their events?

___

3. If you could, what would you speak about?

___

4. What awards do they have?

___

5. If there was an industry association in your area of expertise, what would it be? If it doesn't exist, what would you call it?

___

6. What industry leaders do you admire and why?

___

7. What do they do to advance the agenda of the industry?

_____
_____
_____

8. What are your biggest frustrations with the industry?

_____
_____
_____

9. If you had your way, what would you do?

_____
_____
_____

10. What aspects of the industry are changing for the better?

_____
_____
_____

11. What threats do you see the industry facing?

_____
_____
_____

12. What will this mean for customers?

_____
_____
_____

13. What will this mean for those working in the industry?

_____
_____
_____

14. If you were the best in your industry, what would be happening? What would you be seeing and doing? Who would you be hanging out with?

___

15. What did you feel imagining that experience? Excited? Scared? Nervous?

___

16. How many people could be impacted by your work?

___

17. Why does what you do matter today?

___

18. To move towards this, what would you need to start doing?

___

19. What would you need to stop doing?

___

20. What would you need to continue doing?

___

CHAPTER 3.4

CHAPTER 4
Leverage

"The hours that ordinary people waste, extraordinary people leverage."
– Robin Sharma

You need to leverage to elevate. As an Influencer, the only work you should be doing is thinking, selling and delivering. Everything else – other than some time strategically managing your business – should be delegated. To get the most impact out of everything you do, look for ways to leverage.

The definition of leverage on BusinessDictionary.com is: "The ability to influence a system, or an environment, in a way that multiplies the outcome of one's efforts without a corresponding increase in the consumption of resources."

Leveraging your work creates a ripple effect. Think of leverage as a cake knife. But unlike your regular cake knife, when you push this cake knife down, it cuts six pieces of cake instead of one. Keep that image in your mind every day. As an Influencer, you want to be able to do something once and have multiple things happen as a result.

For example, every time you generate content, use it more than once. Repurpose and reshape it for a blog. Turn it into a podcast or webcast. Use it for marketing material, social media posts and the basis of a coaching program. The idea is to make the most out of what you've already created for maximum impact.

Thought Leaders Global founder Matt Church discusses this concept in his book, *Sell You're Thoughts*. The following table highlights the differences between a commoditiser and an Influencer – someone who knows how to leverage their time, team and thoughts to full effect.

CHAPTER 4

COMMODITISER VS INFLUENCER

	TIME	TEAM	THOUGHTS
COMMODITISER	• Deliver • Sell	• Business to sell	• Finding & repeating
INFLUENCER	• Think • Sell • Deliver	• Practice to grow	• Creating & repurposing

A **commoditiser** focuses so much of their time on delivery and selling, they don't have time for thinking or creating their own positioning and branding. It could also be that they have no desire to create their own thought leadership. Ultimately, they are focused on building a business that can be sold. The drawback of this is that they must sell volume to make their income. Rather than thinking and leveraging their thoughts, they are usually thought *repeating*. They rarely create original work. Instead, their focus is on volume and getting plenty of it out there. In terms of a thought leader's practice, you can do more of this once you've built your positioning and you're trying to leverage it. It's not what you should do in the early stages of building your practice and positioning.

On the other hand, an **Influencer** is focused on "think, sell and deliver". Thinking creates their positioning. They can then elevate their positioning by focusing on their team and their practice, which is what differentiates them in their market. An Influencer is always conscious of repurposing, as opposed to repeating, their thoughts. This elevates and gives further credibility to their positioning in their market. It means they always have something unique, relevant, insightful and different to offer their audience.

It's similar to the world of archery. Previously, the more powerful the bow, the more stronger the archer had to be to successfully draw the bow and release the arrow. But with the development of the compound bow, with its utilisation of a system of pulleys and levers, powerful bows could be operated by children through to the elderly. Subsequently, modern archery has progressed as a sport.

The application of leverage (in this case, through simple physics and some mechanical ingenuity) has enabled archers to significantly leverage their own strength and ability.

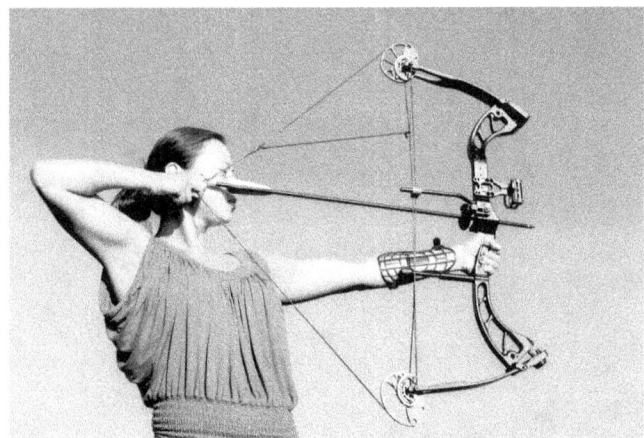
Compound bow.

So, be productive and inventive with your time and resources. What leverage systems and processes do you use each day? What do you do each morning to set yourself up for success every day? What are your habits and routines? What do you do that can be batched and leveraged with your team?

CHAPTER 4

> *Relationships are leverage. If you give value to someone else first, you have leverage.*
>
> — GARY VAYNERCHUK

QUESTIONS FOR YOU TO CONSIDER:

1. What are the most leveraged activities in your day?

___

2. What are the least leveraged?

___

3. Of those that are least leveraged, what can you delegate?

___

4. Of those that are most leveraged, do you maximise them by including them as routines in your schedule?

___

5. If you could wave your magic wand, what would you leverage better?

___

6. Do you see yourself writing and creating your own original content?

___

7. Have you ever sold and marketed an idea before?

___

CHAPTER 4

8. What is your experience in commercial sales?

   _____
   _____
   _____

9. Who do you know that would buy what you sell?

   _____
   _____
   _____

10. Can you see yourself doing the work you're doing now when you're much older?

    _____
    _____
    _____

11. What do you do when you compete on price with your clients?

    _____
    _____
    _____

12. What ways do you currently use to grow your business?

    _____
    _____
    _____

13. How well are they serving you?

    _____
    _____
    _____

14. How do you grow and share your online presence with your own content?

    _____
    _____
    _____

CHAPTER 4.1

Time

"Never mistake motion for action."
– Ernest Hemingway

TRACTION: The force that causes a moving thing to stick against the surface it is moving along.

I was sitting at my desk in my office on a Saturday, in the middle of the day. I was designing and finishing the time management program I was going to deliver the following week. I knew I wasn't going to have enough time to finish it during the week. I remember thinking, "This is ridiculous. How am I supposed to deliver a time management program when here I am on a weekend designing it?"

I realised that something was wrong. Whatever I was doing wasn't working. So, I decided to get a coach.

It was one of the best decisions I've made. The time management lessons I learnt from my coach were life changing. So much so, I went on to work as the lead consultant for a consulting company for five years. I coached and trained teams, CEOs and executive assistants in how to be more productive with their time. I went on to train thousands of people. I delivered my productivity coaching across businesses, the military, federal government and some of the biggest organisations on the planet, including Virgin and Rio Tinto.

After one of my coaching sessions, someone said to me, "You know, this must be really easy for you. You're super organised."

The reality is that I am not a naturally organised person. I like to be organised, and I get frustrated when I'm not, but I'm a go-with-the-flow kind of person, too. I'm spontaneous, I like to jump on ideas, and I'm creative. I have always grappled with finding a balance between these parts of my personality and being organised.

I said to this person, "Do you know what? I'm actually not very organised. I'm more creative with heaps of ideas that easily distract me. But implementing the principles that I do, they help keep the wheels on. Because if I don't follow these processes, the wheels fall off, I don't get to achieve what I want, and I don't feel fulfilled. When I follow the productivity principles I talk about, my days flow far more easily."

Trust me, I'm not always perfect at managing my time. In fact, time management was my failing until I got help from my coach and started to teach others. And, after all the thousands of people I've coached, I've found that there's more to time management and productivity than simply putting procedures in place. It's about identifying a person's natural work flow and deciding what systems best suit them.

There is no one-size-fits-all approach. The goal is to reduce the amount of effort it takes to implement the productivity systems that will work for you.

Time management is such a key part of your success as an Influencer. It's what gives you traction in your business. Often, you will have limited staff. To save time, you may outsource some components of your business. But ultimately, it's up to you to manage all the moving parts. You must be in control.

Sometimes, it feels like time is a conveyor belt. It keeps moving, even though you might want it to stop. The key is to stay ahead of the game so you don't fall behind your competitors. The trouble is, we often overestimate what we can get done in a day and underestimate what we can get done in a lifetime. As the saying goes, "We all have the same amount of hours in a day as Beyoncé." So, make the most of them.

Here are some effective mindset principles to help you get the most out of your time:

- **You are in control.** Simply because someone else wants you to do something doesn't mean you have to. You have the power to manage your time and say no. If you don't take control of your time, someone else will.

- **Clear the clutter.** The cleaner your office is, the better. Clear decisions are made with a clear mind. Too much clutter on your desk and in your work space creates brain fuzz, so keep things tidy.

- **Positive self-talk.** Stop putting yourself down, and catch yourself when you do. Know that you're worthy of success and that you're capable of achieving it. It will help keep you focused so you get more done.

- **Use mind games.** If you want to be the best in the world, pretend you already are! It's amazing what you can achieve when you change your thinking patterns. Before beach volleyball champions Natalie Cook and Kerri

Pottharst won gold at the 2000 Sydney Olympics, their coach had made them fill cabinets in their homes with gold medals borrowed from friends. This made them feel as though they'd already won. So, behave like you've already achieved your goal. Shift your mindset from believing to *being*.

In the words of motivational speaker Paul J. Meyer, "Productivity is never an accident. It is always the result of commitment to excellence, intelligent planning and focused effort."

HOW TO LEVERAGE YOUR TIME TO GET TRACTION

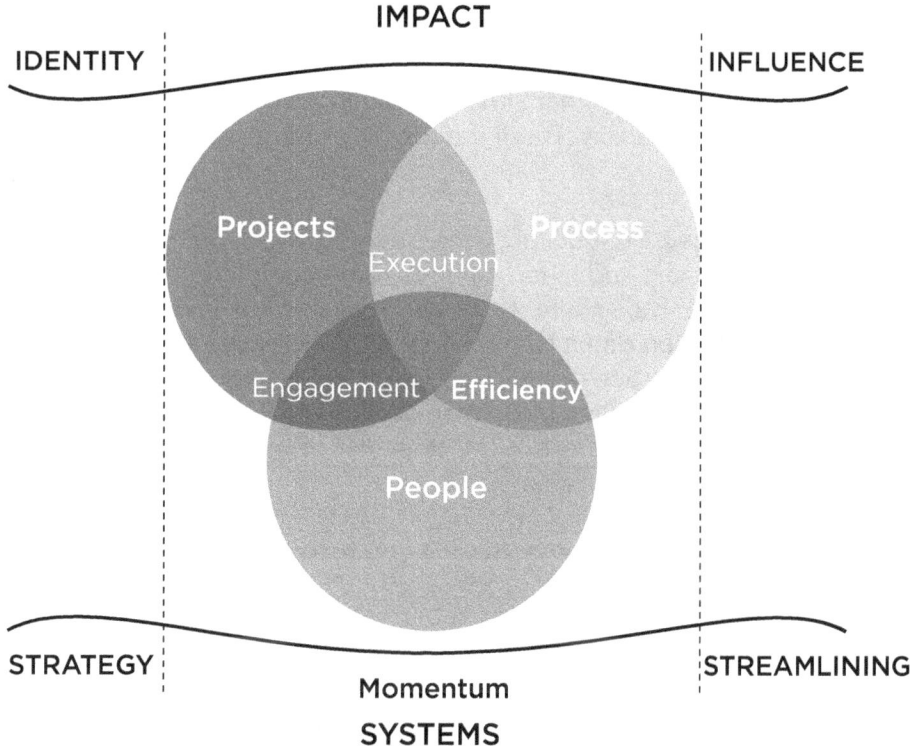

Leveraged time means traction. The three elements that contribute to this traction are **projects, processes** and **people**.

PROJECTS

When you take on a project, you need to know how to allocate your time to get the job done. If you don't make projects a priority by marking them in your calendar and diary, you'll never get started. Break projects up into chunks and ensure that you're working on the right step at the right time.

CHAPTER 4.1

In his landmark text, *The 7 Habits of Highly Effective People*, Stephen R. Covey talks about prioritising the "big rocks" – what is really important to you in life and business. These are your big-picture projects, as opposed to the "gravel and sand" – the smaller, often more pressing issues. To make sure you take care of the big rocks in your business, you need to:

- **Be strategic.** Ensure the projects you have planned align with your goals. This reduces the tendency to chase shiny new objects, helping you stay focused on the things that will get you the most return.

- **Break projects into small steps.** When it comes to big projects, sometimes it can be hard to know where to start. David Allen, productivity expert and author of *Getting Things Done*, says this is because you can't "do" a project. You can only do a physical action. Allen says all projects should start with the question, "What's the next action?" By dividing projects into small, manageable steps, you will reduce time spent procrastinating and get the job done.

- **Start and end dates.** Projects are time oriented. Work out when your project needs to start and when it needs to be completed. Once you have broken the project into smaller tasks, work backwards in your calendar, allocating completion dates for those tasks. That way, you will have a timeframe you must stick to. You'll probably realise you have a lot less time to get all your projects done than you previously thought. Instead of complaining that you don't have the time and dropping the project, look at your calendar and make the time.

- **Delegate.** When you can, get someone you trust to take on some of the steps involved in your project.

- **Allocate time in your calendar for bigger pieces of work.** If something's not getting done, it's probably because it's still on a to-do list. It needs to be in your calendar. If a job is going to take more than 10 minutes, work out how much time it will take, then allocate that time in your diary or calendar.

PROCESSES

Processes are your daily, weekly and monthly habits and routines. For example, you may answer emails at a certain time each day, batch meetings at a certain time of month, and do particular tasks on certain days. Routines give structure to your work, allowing you to have greater control over your business and success as an Influencer.

Charles Duhigg, the bestselling author of *The Power of Habit*, says that creating habits around processes and routines requires less energy, willpower and discipline. Once these habits have been created, your energy goes into the more challenging aspects of your practice.

Here are some simple yet effective practices that will improve your efficiency:

- **Inbox processing times rather than checking your email all day.** When you're trying to concentrate on a task, it is extremely distracting to constantly receive email notifications. Go into your inbox settings and turn them off. Allocate specific times during the day to check your emails so you don't get sidetracked every few minutes.

- **Identify habits and routines.** Certain tasks will need to be addressed every day, week, month or year. Identify these tasks and calendarise them. Dealing with tasks proactively rather than reactively will save you time and headaches.

- **Capture your ideas.** It's easy to lose track of ideas if you don't write them down. According to productivity author Tony Schwarz, people can only hold seven items in their working memory at once. Hold onto your ideas by using tools such as Memo Mailer, a digital audio voice recorder. Save them into an ideas folder on your desktop, and record them in your diary or calendar.

- **Batch tasks.** Dedicating blocks of time to similar tasks is an efficient way of getting jobs done. It maximises your concentration and decreases the chance of procrastination. If you have multiple 10-minute jobs to do, schedule an hour to get them all done. If you find yourself with some spare time during the day, use it to get a head start.

- **Meetings.** Most meetings are a complete waste of time and don't have enough conscious thought. The key is to ensure they're a conscious choice, not something you do because they're part of your routine. When you're in a fast-growth phase, regular and shorter meetings generally work better than longer and irregular ones. Using them to innovate and fine tune can be powerful.

- **Create before you consume.** Marie Forleo, the founder of B-School and bestselling author, says spending too much time on social media reading other people's work is the fastest way to reduce the growth of your practice. As a thought leader, you need to be writing content far more than you consume it. So, start your days creating content and watch your practice thrive.

CHAPTER 4.1

- **Planning time.** Jeff Bezos, the founder and CEO of Amazon.com, realised he needed more thinking time. He allocates two hours per day to simply think. Most of the executives I work with don't have enough thinking time allocated in their calendars. They come from a managing mindset, where they've been 100% busy implementing rather than allocating time for strategising. Your brain needs to rest and a chance to get creative to undertake the work that you do.

PEOPLE

Procrastination is the undoing of so much potential. It's often what we do when we're feeling overwhelmed. Research shows that entrepreneurs work an average of 52 hours per week, which is 63% longer than the average worker.[1] In my experience, entrepreneurs work even longer than that – particularly in the start-up phase of their business.

As an Influencer, you are incredibly busy. You can't do it all alone. Otherwise, you risk burning out. To get traction, to move forward instead of merely spinning the wheels, you need to tap into the personalities, skills and thinking of others. It will take the pressure off and give your business momentum.

When utilising the skills of others, consider the following:

- **Meetings.** Are you having the right meetings with the right people? Or are you having meetings for the sake of it? If they aren't brainstorming or decision-making meetings, it's time to question their effectiveness and if they are truly needed.

- **Follow up.** When you delegate tasks to others, keep tabs on their progress. Although you have delegated the task, you are still accountable for it. Use collaboration and task-tracking tools, such as Trello, Slack and Taskworld.

- **Give feedback.** It's important you give the people you work with direction. Let them know when things are going well and when they aren't. By having these conversations early, you can save yourself a lot of time later on.

- **Batch conversations.** People are like dump trucks, always looking to dump stuff on you and creating interruptions. I had a client, David, who was interrupted all day and then started his work at 5pm after everyone went home. Needless to say, he was not able to spend quality time with his family or look after himself by getting in some exercise. He was also frustrated because he was unable to read his kids a book before they went

---

[1] "How Many Hours Should You Work Each Week?" *Inc.*, September 26, 2014, https://www.inc.com/john-rampton/what-hours-should-i-work-everyday-as-an-entrepreneur.html

to bed. So, we created a "call-in time" between 4pm and 5pm each day for his team. As a result, they found the answers to their questions throughout the day and it reduced the amount of questions he was asked by about one quarter. So, look for ways to batch your team's interruptions. Set proactive times with them if you need to.

- **Debriefing.** My friend Christian "Boo" Boucousis is a former fighter pilot and an expert in leadership and productivity. In his keynotes, he talks about how fighter pilots brief and debrief their missions. The debrief is considered just as important as the mission itself. It's the same in your practice. Constant improvement, learning and refining are key to high performance and a powerful practice. This means debriefing the logistics of an event you spoke at, the way your social media accounts are run and your training programs.

Other factors that can influence your ability to leverage your time include:

- **Identity.** The personalities of the people you work with can help or hinder your time management. Ensure you have the right people in your practice. Your recruitment processes and the way you choose vendors are important.

- **Impact.** Is the work you're undertaking achieving the results you and your clients are looking for? What results are you getting? Do you need to focus on work that makes more of an impact?

- **Influence.** Do you have the influence you want with your team and clients? Are you being heard? Is your message clear? How seriously do people take you and how do you get them to do what you want them to do?

- **Strategy.** Identify your goals. What are you trying to achieve? What's your focus? Does your team understand your vision and are they on board?

- **Systems.** What systems, procedures and checklists do you have in place so your business continues to grow? If something isn't working, you must be able to identify it and rectify it. Taking personal responsibility to improve, even just a little bit each day, makes a big difference in the long run.

- **Streamlining.** Having a mindset of continuous improvement matters in this game. Once you have the systems in place, it's about improving those systems so they are seamless. You have to reduce the amount of friction in them as much as possible. After each project or challenging situation, debrief with your team to find better ways to execute your systems and strategies. It will create less pressure and stress for you. Think of it as ensuring your oxygen mask is on all the time.

> *The way we measure productivity is flawed. People checking their BlackBerry over dinner is not the measure of productivity.*
>
> **— TIMOTHY FERRISS**

QUESTIONS FOR YOU TO CONSIDER:

1. How often do you plan your week, month, quarter and year?

___

2. Have you got too much on your plate? What do you need to remove?

___

3. Who can you delegate some tasks to?

___

4. What tasks need to be done every day, week, month or year?

___

5. When will you put those habits and routines in your calendar or communicate them to your staff?

___

6. How many procedures do you have in your practice? Who is responsible for looking after them?

___

7. Do you set aside at least one hour of your day for dealing with unexpected issues?

8. When you need total focus, who do you divert your phone to?

9. What system do you have in place if you must address something urgently?

10. How do you ensure procedures are maintained?

11. Write down your top three projects for the next week. How long will each task take and when will you do them?

12. Have you put them in your calendar? If not, do it now.

13. What motivation tools and techniques do you use to keep yourself focused and on task?

TIME

14. What three goals do you aim to achieve this quarter?

___

15. What big three goals do you aim to achieve this year?

___

16. How do you manage interruptions from your team?

___

17. Do you schedule regular meetings with your team? How often? Twice daily? Weekly?

___

18. What do you do to ensure you are put first as the most important customer?

___

19. How do you ensure you don't attend meetings that are a waste of time?

___

20. How do you ensure your team is prepared for their meetings with you?

___

CHAPTER 4.1

CHAPTER 4.2

Content

"Content builds relationships. Relationships are built on trust. Trust drives revenue."
– Andrew Davis, author of Brandscaping

Leveraged thoughts amplify your brand and your positioning. So, once you're clear on your message, you can build your business more quickly by leveraging your thoughts.

When it comes to leveraging content, remember to think once and use often. It's like using a blueprint. For example, builders such as G.J. Gardner Homes and AVJennings don't design a house from scratch every time they build. They work from blueprints. They may tweak a blueprint and customise it where necessary, but they use the same blueprint to build thousands of homes. You can do the same with your content to save time and energy.

Sharing the same message in multiple ways – blog posts, webcasts, podcasts, books – is an efficient way of reaching more people. It creates a ripple effect: you'll make more of an impact on a wider audience and amplify your thought leadership more quickly.

In the past, to build your profile and positioning you needed to get a column in a newspaper or magazine. You needed your manuscript to be accepted by a publisher before you could get your book published.

It's very different now. Social media allows you to share your content whenever you want. You can publish your own book with ease, and at a relatively low cost. Anyone has the potential to become a household name. How many times have you seen unknowns gain sudden fame through a YouTube video?

Bernard Salt is, essentially, the rainmaker for KPMG. He is a keynote speaker, business adviser and columnist who has channeled social media to really cement his positioning as the leader in his field. His insights form the foundation of KPMG Demographics' success.

Naomi Simson is another entrepreneur who has harnessed the power of social media. Founding director of online experience gift retailer RedBalloon, she is the number-one Australian Influencer on LinkedIn, with more 1.5 million LinkedIn followers.

So, as a result of their blogging and speaking, these two industry giants have created another platform that helps them grow their businesses.

However, seeking fame is not what being an Influencer is all about. As discussed in an article in the *Australian Financial Review*,[1] it's possible to leverage content to, and be an Influencer for, smaller groups and markets. You don't have to be known by the masses to be a thought leader. Seeking fame is driven by ego, not the desire to help others. Providing the very best solutions to people's problems should underpin everything you say and do as an Influencer.

Have faith in your message and content. Experts are often held back by a lack of self-confidence – particularly women. They're concerned their voice will only add to the noise. "What am I going to talk about? What if people don't want to listen?" But leveraging your content is essential to your success as an Influencer.

The people who buy from you are the people who know you. And to get them to know you, you need to reach out to them with your content. In his book *Linchpin: Are You Indispensable?*, Seth Godin says the people who succeed in business are the linchpins – the ones who nurture tribes. They do this by seeking connections in an authentic way and sharing their "art" with others. In other words, they reach out to people and grow their business through influence: sharing helpful, inspiring content.

What's more, as we've mentioned previously, it's estimated that by 2019, content marketing will be a $300 billion industry.[2] It's certainly no fad!

You can leverage your content across so many online and offline platforms, including:

- Blogs
- Videos
- Newsletters
- Podcasts
- Training courses
- Webinars
- Keynotes

---

[1] "The Rise of Brand Me." *Australian Financial Review*, November 3, 2015, http://www.afr.com/leadership/the-rise-of-brand-me-20150923-gjtdsc
[2] "Content marketing will be a $300 billion industry by 2019." *Marketing*, July 10, 2015, https://www.marketingmag.com.au/news-c/content-marketing-will-300-billion-industry-2019/

- Book chapters
- E-books
- Workshops
- Seminars

CHAPTER 4.2

QUESTIONS FOR YOU TO CONSIDER:

1. What social platforms have you established?

_____
_____
_____
_____

2. How many social followers do you have on each platform, especially on LinkedIn?

_____
_____
_____
_____

3. Who else blogs about your subject?

_____
_____
_____

4. What insights do they have?

_____
_____
_____

5. How often do you write content?

_____
_____
_____

6. What do you like about the ideas others have in your space? What do you disagree with?

_____
_____
_____

7. How can you incorporate what's being said into your own content?

_____
_____
_____

8. If I was to audit you, how many pieces or original content would you have created?

_____
_____

9. If each piece of content was worth $10,000 before it's even been used, what would the value of your IP asset base be right now?

_____
_____
_____

10. What would it take to increase it?

_____
_____
_____

11. Write down a list of each article on your thought leadership that you can post. How many times can each piece of content be shared before going into a book or program? Consider Facebook, LinkedIn, Twitter, podcast and video. There are so many possibilities!

_____
_____
_____
_____

12. Have you allocated time to record your content? (Hint: An efficient way of doing this is to write down your points, stories, facts, case studies and evidence. Use this content to create a podcast, then transcribe it and use the content for your blog and then your book.)

_____
_____

13. Have you allocated time to batch film your videos? Have you prepared and practiced your scripts to save time and money when working with your videographer?

___

14. Have you allocated time to batch record your podcasts? When will you do your practice run? Have you tested all your equipment?

___

15. Who will edit your videos and podcasts? Will you need to do them?

___

16. What other platforms do you need to add to your content planner?

___

17. Who can you engage to delegate the roll-out of your content across all platforms?

___

18. What online training courses or chapters in books are you planning to write that you could use for your podcasts and videos to save time later?

___

19. What recording app have your got installed on your phone to record your keynotes and workshops for more content?

_____
_____
_____
_____

20. Have you practiced getting your videos down to one minute so they can be easily shared across all platforms, including Instagram?

_____
_____
_____
_____

CHAPTER 4.2

CHAPTER 4.3
People

"The potential of the average person is like a huge ocean unsailed, a new continent unexplored, a world of possibilities waiting to be released and channeled toward some great good."
– Brian Tracy

Some of your greatest resources come from the people around you. You cannot build a successful Influencer business on your own. You need help and support. By surrounding yourself with a team of professionals, by delegating to them and leveraging their skills, you not only save time; you give yourself a greater chance of success.

To leverage your team, you need to tap into their skills, personalities and interests. Personality tests are a great way of identifying the traits and qualities you can leverage. The Myers-Briggs Type Indicator® and DiSC® personality profile are two easily accessible personality tests. Tom Rath's book *StrengthsFinder 2.0* is another helpful way of identifying certain personality types. The Fascination Personality Test, created by branding expert and author Sally Hogshead, is also worth exploring.

Once you've identified your team's personalities and strengths, nurture them. Help them grow. By helping your team reach their potential, they will feel fulfilled by the work they do for you and your business will benefit.

A couple of years ago, I ran a group session at a financial services firm. I conducted a survey of the workers, which revealed that one group scored particularly low on happiness at work. Interestingly, many of the people in this group had been identified as low performers by the organisation. This same group scored highly for money as their key driver. Money became a way for them to feel compensated for disliking their work so much.

When your team is passionate about the work they do for you, the quality of their performance skyrockets. Therefore, it's so important that your team feels happy, validated and encouraged by you.

In her book *Happiness at Work: Maximizing Your Psychological Capital for Success*, Jessica Pryce-Jones – chair and founder of the iOpener Institute –

explores the secrets of being happy at work and why it's important in human and financial terms. She identifies the five components of the happiness-at-work equation:

- **Contribution.** Your team members need to feel as though they're making a difference. They must see a direct correlation between what they're doing and where the organisation is heading. Give your team members clear goals and objectives, and provide them with feedback, so they feel their role is important and valued.

- **Confidence.** Let your team members know that they're doing a great job. Increase their confidence by giving them tasks that push the boundaries of their comfort zone. Always be there to support and guide them, especially when tackling something new.

- **Conviction.** This is about ensuring your team members are motivated in their role. They need to feel effective and efficient: "I know what I'm doing." Conviction also means being resilient during more challenging times.

- **Commitment.** This is achieved when your team has a sense of purpose and loyalty. It's particularly important to get through the tough days. Build a strong, authentic connection with your team members so they feel as though they belong and don't look for work elsewhere.

- **Culture.** This is made up of the norms, practices and behaviours of your work environment. When you have a positive and efficient work culture, your team members are more likely to enjoy their jobs, which means they'll perform better. Treat your team fairly. Give them autonomy with their roles so they feel valued.

Overarching these five components is your team's need for a sense of **pride, trust,** and **recognition** in the job as well.

So, take the time to look after your team. Make the most of their skills and personalities, but also ensure you give back so they feel truly valued and committed to your cause.

QUESTIONS FOR YOU TO CONSIDER:

1. What aspects of your work truly require you and no one else to do them?

___

2. What tasks can be delegated to make better use of your team?

___

3. What tasks could be outsourced to staff overseas?

___

4. What tasks could you delegate to a virtual assistant (VA) locally, even if it's only for a few hours per week?

___

5. What are the career aspirations of your team? What does potential look like for them?

___

6. What are your team's interests outside of work?

___

CHAPTER 4.3

7. What does their dream month look like?

8. Who are their heroes?

9. What are their strengths?

10. If they had the opportunity to learn more, what would they choose to learn?

11. In what areas of their roles do your team members feel most confident?

12. In what areas are they not so confident?

13. Which area is of highest priority to help them improve?

14. What do you need to do to help them with this?

_____
_____
_____

15. What do you think motivates your team? What would they say?

_____
_____
_____

16. In what areas do your team members feel they contribute the most?

_____
_____
_____

17. On a scale of 1 to 10, how committed is your team to your mission?

_____
_____
_____

18. On a scale of 1 to 10, how much would you say your team is heard? How do you ensure your team feels heard?

_____
_____
_____

19. As a leader, how often do you ask for feedback from your team?

_____
_____
_____

20. How often do you ask your team what you can do to make their job easier?

_____
_____
_____

CHAPTER 4.3

CHAPTER 5

Lead Generation

"To be an influencer, you have to love people before you can try to lead them."
– John Maxwell

The customer journey has changed.

While the concept of marketing and how it leads into the customer sales experience hasn't changed too much, the mechanics of it have. According to a study by McKinsey, 10 years ago the average consumer wanting to purchase a vehicle would visit five car dealerships. Today, the consumer visits 1.6.[1]

This figure reflects the explosion of information on the internet. Consumers are now able to do so much of their research about products and services online, they don't need to step into a bricks-and-mortar store or office. Buyers are making decisions about you, your services and how you help them all the time – and you may not even be aware of it.

Let's look at what I call the Lead Generation model within the business environment of the past, then within the business environment of the present.

THE PRE-DIGITAL CUSTOMER JOURNEY

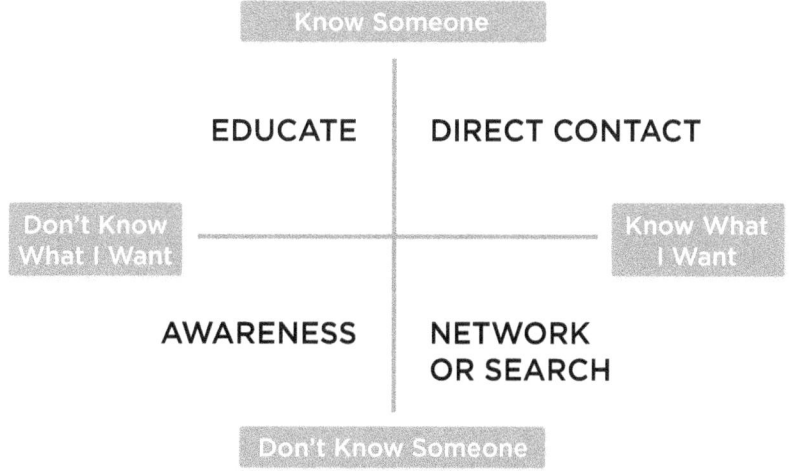

---

[1] "Americans rethinking how they buy cars." CNBC, February 25, 2014, http://www.cnbc.com/2014/02/26/americans-rethinking-how-they-buy-cars.html

CHAPTER 5

DIRECT CONTACT

"I know someone who can help me and I know what I want."

In the past, customers sought the services of people they remembered. They knew what they wanted and they knew who could help them. From a business perspective, you also knew your customers and understood their needs. You might have had a customer database, even if it was a file of cards!

Direct contact was a highly effective way of doing business. When I managed a retail shoe store, I kept a list of customers with details on their shoes size and the brands they loved. I fondly remember a customer called Mrs Thomas, who always bought size 9 shoes and loved a brand called Lorbac. They were beautiful shoes and always fitted her perfectly. A pair of Lorbac shoes cost about $300, and each season I would set aside every size 9 pair of Lorbac shoes that came in and call Mrs Thomas. She always bought them all! And throughout the year, whenever Mrs Thomas needed a new pair of shoes, she knew she could call me to see if I had anything that would suit her. I knew her and she knew me. Sometimes, I would even see things in other stores she might like and let her know about them. I didn't receive any commission on sales, but it helped that I knew her likes and dislikes. She trusted my taste and I didn't waste her time.

NETWORK OR SEARCH

"I don't know someone who can help me, but I know what I want."

In the past, if a customer needed help with something but didn't know who to turn to, they would either ask their network – usually family and friends – for recommendations, or open the phone book and do a search.

The advice from family and friends was based on brand recall from magazine, television and radio advertising. This meant that trying to remain top of mind was an expensive exercise for businesses.

In terms of search, businesses needed to be as close to the top of the listings in the phone book as possible. Many businesses opted for names that started with "A" – for example, Aardvark Consulting – so customers were more likely to see them first. This was the equivalent of today's organic Google search. Think of paying for a big ad in the phone book like investing in Google AdWords today.

AWARENESS

"I don't know someone who can help me and I don't know what I want."

In a pre-digital world, to get in front of the people you didn't know and who didn't know you, you had to invest in media advertising, billboards, public relations campaigns and cold calling. Creating awareness was a lengthy, expensive process.

Speaking was also part of this process and there was a heavy emphasis on getting in front of new clients. Today, we have much higher return on activities where people already know us, such as working with our databases. US marketing guru Seth Godin really pioneered public speaking for business with his books *Permission Marketing* and *Tribes*.

EDUCATE

"I know who can help me but I don't know what I want."

This quadrant represents the greatest shift in the customer journey. In the pre-digital world, businesses had mailing lists – but the way they educated the people on these lists was with print material, such as newsletters, flyers and catalogues. The problem was, these were rarely educational or interesting. Newsletters were also often done half-heartedly and irregularly. They failed to effectively target and educate those people who were aware of the business, but didn't realise they had a problem that needed solving.

POST DIGITAL

To achieve a competitive edge in business today, you need to stand out from the crowd. But you need to stand out in a meaningful, authentic way. You need to be an Influencer and make an impact.

But what, exactly, does being an Influencer mean?

WHAT IS AN INFLUENCER?

Influencers have the power to lead, set direction for others and affect purchasing decisions. They do this using their wealth of expertise, credibility and positioning. An Influencer does not hustle people into buying or coerce them into doing as they say; rather, an Influencer acts straight from the heart.

An Influencer genuinely wants to help others. They want to see their customers and potential clients flourish, both in their businesses and personal lives. They are generous with the wisdom they share and do not ask for anything in return. As well as investing in their own learning, they empower others to learn, too.

They build trust easily and deliver what they say they will. They are well connected and add value to conversations in their industry, often setting new directions and creating new ideas. They are forward thinking and aren't afraid to challenge the status quo. They are sought after for their advice, knowledge and leadership. And they often have a loyal social media following.

It takes courage to be an Influencer. You need to have a strong belief in yourself and in what you offer. It's not always easy and it takes time. But it's vital to cutting through the noise and ensuring you are at the forefront of your audience's mind.

The benefits are not all abstract, either. Your sales will skyrocket. Here's why.

WHY BECOME AN INFLUENCER?

It's true that as an Influencer, you cannot expect anything in return for what you do. You cannot share your knowledge and guide others with the expectation they will pay for it. There must be a genuine desire to help others. And you must find true reward in knowing you are making a difference to the lives of others through education.

But, by its very nature, being an Influencer invites wonderful things to come your way.

Sales are an organic element of being an Influencer. People want to connect and work with people they can trust. In fact, a study released by *Forbes* found that 43% of millennials – one of the largest and most influential demographic cohorts – rank authenticity over content when consuming news.[2] *Forbes* says: "They first have to trust a company or news site before they even bother reading the content that they produce." Furthermore, only 1% of millennials surveyed said that a compelling advertisement would make them trust a brand more. This is because they believe "advertising is all spin and not authentic". Rather, they review blogs before making a purchase. Thirty-three percent of those surveyed said they read blogs before making a purchasing decision, compared to 3% who said they relied on information from TV news, magazines or books before deciding to buy.

---

2 "10 New Findings About the Millennial Consumer." *Forbes*, 2015, http://www.forbes.com/sites/danschawbel/2015/01/20/10-new-findings-about-the-millennial-consumer/#d361a8328a87

So, it pays to be an Influencer. People want to work with people who are authentic – people who they know, like and trust. In this digital age where there is so much information and so much choice available to them, people want meaningful relationships. They want to connect with you. Engage them meaningfully, and you will be rewarded with their loyalty.

HOW DO YOU BECOME AN INFLUENCER?

To become an Influencer, you must connect with and engage your audience. It's no use having endless knowledge and game-changing ideas for your industry, yet being unable to reach out to people.

Some people seem to have an innate ability to hit it off with everyone. They have that charisma that draws people in and are unselfconscious when it comes to putting themselves out there. But for many people, connecting with others is hard work – especially if you're not used to it!

The good news is that *anyone* can have that impact. What you need is commitment. A commitment to take the initiative, start the conversations and keep the momentum going. A commitment to continuously improve your game and educate others in a way that will change their lives. The more you do these things, the easier they will become.

So, how do you get started? You need a plan of action. And that plan of action is explained in the Lead Generation for Thought Leaders model.

LEAD GENERATION IN THE NEW WORLD OF BUSINESS

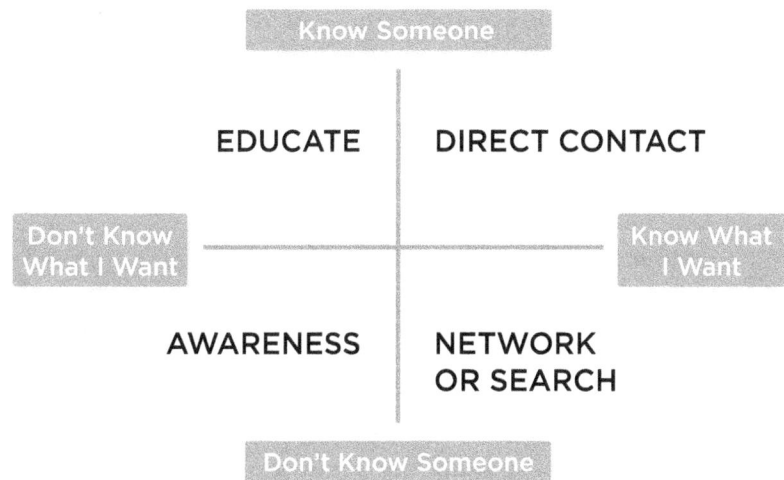

CHAPTER 5

The Lead Generation in the New World of Business model provides you with real, actionable steps to take you from expert to Influencer. It will ensure that people not only find you, but want to work with you.

Notice it is the same model as the pre-digital customer journey, but with the influence of digital, social media, technology and new communication platforms, the dynamics of each quadrant work quite differently. Hence, positioning yourself as an Influencer allows you to dominate each quadrant with more ease, trust and growth.

The model contains the following quadrants:

- **Direct Contact**
- **Network or Search**
- **Awareness**
- **Educate**

Each quadrant consists of three activities you must undertake to build your positioning as an Influencer. These activities will be explained in further detail in the coming chapters of this book.

The model also considers the four types of potential clients out there:

- People who know someone
- People who know what they want
- People who don't know someone
- People who don't know what they want

Let's examine these four types of consumer and how they relate to the different quadrants of the model.

DIRECT CONTACT

"I know someone who can help me and I know what I want."

This type of customer already knows who you are. They know you offer what they need. But for them to take that next step and call you or email you, you must be at the front of their mind. So, it's important you keep in regular contact.

As an Influencer, you will generally need to communicate with them at least once per week until you have a solid footing in your market. Solid footing is when you're turning over about $650,000-plus per year. Anything below that, or if you are accessing a new type of client, means you will need to ramp up your communication. Most entrepreneurs don't communicate enough and are afraid of annoying people, being "spammy" and communicating so much that people unsubscribe. Yet, it's not unusual for Influencers in the US to communicate daily or at least three times per week via email.

A great example of someone who leverages direct contact effectively is Nikki Fogden-Moore, an expert in vitality who is based on the Sunshine Coast in Queensland, Australia. Nikki specialises in working with super-busy executives and entrepreneurs who are tired, lacking energy and balance. Each Monday, she sends them an email that she calls her "Monday Mojo". It's a wonderful email to receive first thing each week and puts a spring in the receiver's step.

Building your client database is critical to keeping in touch. Your database can include existing clients, people you've met or groups of people with a common interest or problem. You need to reach out to your database regularly to maintain visibility. The idea is that you come immediately to mind when they need you, or when someone they know needs someone like you.

Direct Contact is the most valuable quadrant of the model. Building your client database requires plenty of groundwork and you must keep at it day in, day out. But the benefits are enormous. As Seth Godin says: "The people who will buy from you are those who know you."

NETWORK OR SEARCH

"I don't know someone who can help me, but I know what I want."

In this situation, the potential client will seek recommendations. If they're extroverted or well-networked, they will consult their colleagues and friends for referrals, as they trust them. If they're more introverted, they will conduct an online search. Sometimes, people will do both.

Being referred by a network is ideal. It means you have a good reputation, and when you have a good reputation you have solid positioning. It makes your job of finding new clients so much easier. Knowing who your current and potential key referrers are is crucial. Once you know who they are, you can apply specific strategies to reward and encourage them further.

A good example of this is an insolvency firm we recently worked with. The field of financial planning, accounting and insolvency is often very complicated and requires a high level of knowledge, so the average consumer doesn't know what to do if their business becomes insolvent. Their first port of call will usually be a lawyer or accountant, who will then call an insolvency firm. Most business owners won't go directly to an insolvency agency, as it's so specialised. Essentially, insolvency firms are *known for knowing something*. They're Influencers in their field. So, in your business, you really want to be become like an insolvency firm: specialised, respected and easily referred. We'll cover some of the strategies these agencies use so that you, too, can use them to get referrals and greater positioning as an Influencer.

Being found on the top page of a Google search result is often considered to be the "nirvana" of business growth. For an Influencer's practice, however, this isn't always the case. Often, the potential client doing the search doesn't know you. If no one has referred you to them, it's difficult for you to stand out. You'll be competing with all the other people and businesses that come up in the search – some of whom may have more experience with search engine optimisation and Google AdWords than you. This means they will appear higher in the search results list than you, and the closer a business is to the top, the more likely the potential client will click on their link.

In a Google search, you'll look the same as everybody else – rather like toothpaste on a supermarket shelf. It's hard to sell your defining features and uniqueness in that space. You'll be competing on price, and that's a difficult space in which to sell. While your buyer may be ready, you need to be able to compete aggressively to stand out when you're found. This can be difficult to do when you're an Influencer. Nevertheless, it's important that we discuss this issue so you know where it fits in an Influencer's business growth process.

However, if you are well networked, your referrals will come to the fore – even in search engine results. If you don't have a LinkedIn profile, set one up now! Ultimately, LinkedIn is a search engine, so it's essential you set up your LinkedIn profile with the right keywords and include testimonials. That way, you'll be more likely to turn up in online search results.

AWARENESS

"I don't know someone who can help me and I don't know what I want."

This activity is designed to access new markets. People in new markets don't know you. They may not have come across your insights, and they may not have even articulated the problems they have that you can solve. Ignorance can be bliss for customers in this quadrant, so you must penetrate the noise they're exposed to and grab their attention.

To engage this type of client, you need to build awareness. Let them know who you are, what you do, who you help and *how* you help. Blog posts, articles, videos, podcasts and social media profiles are all important tools in your awareness arsenal.

The work you do offline is important, too. Public speaking, attending networking events and appearing at expos will help your potential clients get to know you. They will see that while they may not need your help right now, they might down the track – or someone they know will. The goal is to continually be proactive and reach out to others so you can grow your list and start to nurture them.

A great example of this is a client we recently worked with called Adam. He's an expert in creating high-performing schools and learning cultures. He's been so successful with this, he identified that many corporate organisations have the same problems as some of the schools he works with. Adam could see they needed his help, so he decided to take his approach to the corporate market. In terms of getting clients, it was like starting his business all over again. So, we helped Adam access the people who didn't know him and who didn't know they had this problem he could solve. Adam had to be super proactive in reaching out to corporates and educating them about his message.

Advertising, PR and radio are all valuable activities here, but in an Influencer's world, your list is everything. It's so important that you maximise every opportunity to build your list and nurture awareness of what you do. You cannot simply live in the hope that the people on your list will need your help immediately, because it's usually not the case.

Elon Musk is a fantastic example of someone who does this exceptionally well. As the CEO of Tesla and SpaceX, he is renowned for going through PR consultants who don't immediately grasp his vision. He realises the value of raising the awareness of people who don't know him or his message about creating a sustainable planet.

EDUCATE

"I know who can help me but I don't know what I want."

Although they know who you are, these kinds of customers are not aware that they need your help. In this case, it is your job to educate them.

You must regularly create and share content so people understand what you do. By educating them on how you can help them, they may realise they have a problem – they just weren't aware of it until now. People often don't realise they have an issue that needs resolving or an area they could improve on unless someone educates them.

Writing posts, sharing updates and providing insightful comments are simple ways to educate and demonstrate your deep understanding of the problems you solve. The goal of your content is to encourage your audience to think, "Wow, that's exactly what I'm after!" It must provide a clear connection between their problems and your solutions.

The three key drivers of education are:

- **Your book.** The right book will educate and take you where you need to go. Most Influencers write the wrong book – it positions them too low for where they are and where they want to be. Books take effort, time, focus and determination. If it were easy, everyone would be doing it. As comedian Amy Poehler says, "I have told people that writing this book has been like brushing away dirt from a fossil. What a load of sh**. It has been like hacking away at a freezer with a screwdriver."

- **Your productivity.** Productivity means focus and support. It's the ability to get work done, streamline, systemise and replicate. In this industry, there's a real art to getting a balance between creativity and execution, as you're doing lots of creating and implementing at the same time. If you can't follow a calendar, take control of your time and be disciplined, it can easily eat you alive. As Neil Bradman, global marketing expert, says, "Ninety per cent of marketing doesn't work because it doesn't get done."

- **Your insight.** You must know your content and why it matters, and articulate it to your audience. You can't just focus on the *how*. Your audience needs to see the value in your message before you start talking about how you help. The Institute for the Future's Future Work Skills 2020 report identified that one of the key skills for the next five to 10 years is something called "sense-making. This skill is about giving meaning to experience. As an Influencer, when you provide insights or make connections between issues, you demonstrate an understanding that shows mastery and is highly persuasive. It provides your audience with meaning. In the words of Vincent van Gogh, "If one is master of one thing and understands one thing well, one has at the same time, insight into and understanding of many things."

WHERE TO FROM HERE?

As you can see, it's easy to help those you already know. It can be hard work reaching out to people you've never met, creating awareness of what you do and building your networks. But all four quadrants of this model are crucial to becoming an Influencer. And you must work on them every day – not just once or twice a year when you have a spare couple of hours. Everything you do in your business must be linked to this model.

Remember, there is always someone out there trying to find you – even if they don't know it yet!

The following chapters of this book will provide a thorough exploration of each quadrant of the model. You will gain an understanding of all the activities you need to do to ensure you are fulfilling each area and cementing your positioning as an Influencer. These are tried and true activities that have not only formed the foundation of my own career as an Influencer; they have helped my clients become successful Influencers in their fields, too.

So, let's get started on your transformation into an Influencer!

CHAPTER 5

QUESTIONS FOR YOU TO CONSIDER:

1. What aspects of being an Influencer resonate with you? Why?

___

2. Which Influencers or experts in your industry do you admire? Why?

___

3. As an Influencer, what aspects of what they do can you see yourself doing?

___

4. If you grew up before the internet existed, what tools did you use to find goods and services? Friends, family, the phone book, magazines?

___

5. What do you currently do to build awareness with your ideal clients?

___

6. How is this working for you?

___

7. How do you educate the clients who might be considering working with you? How do you give them insights into how you can help them?

_____
_____
_____

8. What do you do to be easily found by your ideal client?

_____
_____
_____

9. Is this working? How do you know?

_____
_____

10. What opportunities do you see to help you grow your Influencer business? What stands out to you?

_____
_____
_____

11. If you were to write a book, what would the title and subtitle be?

_____
_____
_____

12. How do you think this book might help people?

_____
_____
_____

13. How do you know they would buy it? Are people buying similar books on Amazon?

_____
_____

CHAPTER 5

14. On a scale of 1 to 10, how productive are you?
_____
_____

15. What would need to happen for that to improve?
_____
_____
_____

16. How do you teach others to be productive?
_____
_____
_____

17. How often do you find yourself thinking about the meaning behind experiences, ideas and concepts?
_____
_____
_____

18. How do you capture these insights? Do you write them down and share with others if you're asked? Are you consulted for your insights?
_____
_____
_____

19. What is your top insight from this chapter at this point?
_____
_____
_____

20. How do you think you might use this insight?
_____
_____
_____

CHAPTER 5.1
Direct Contact

"It's easier to love a brand when the brand loves you back."
– Seth Godin

We've all been there. That awkward situation where someone has cold called you or flagged you down on the street, trying to sell you something or sign you up to a deal you're not interested in. All you want to do is hang up or run away.

If you think that is what direct contact is about, then put that thought out of your head right now! Direct contact is not about hassling people. It's not about selling yourself and what you offer by shouting through a loudspeaker. It's about communicating effectively. It's about taking a targeted, proactive and insightful approach to educating and informing your clients and leads. And it's about building greater trust and connection with your audience to grow your business.

People are usually unimpressed with a "salesy" approach. When you engage in direct-contact activities, building a client relationship based on trust and respect is paramount. A survey conducted by Concerto Marketing Group and Research Now found that when customers trust a brand, 83% will recommend a trusted company to others and 82% will continue to use that brand frequently.[1] In other words, if you have a great customer relationship that's free of gimmicks and empty promises, your business will grow.

For example, I recently engaged a service provider – an expert, in fact – to help me with improving a process in my business. We were chatting on the phone about the process and everything was going well until the expert said: "I tell my staff that if a customer calls and asks if we can help with something we haven't done before or we're unsure of, just say yes to the customer. We can work it out later."

Wow. I didn't see that coming. In that moment, I lost all trust in the business and the expert. I felt there was a lack of respect. I felt like he didn't understand me, wasn't listening, and lacked the credibility I thought he had.
As bestselling American author Seth Godin says: "The digital asset that

---

[1] "Three Ways to Build Customer Trust." *Forbes*, April 22, 2014, http://www.forbes.com/sites/yec/2014/04/22/three-ways-to-build-customer-trust/#d3a3b4278db5

matters is trust. Awareness first, then interaction, and maybe a habit, but all three mean nothing if they don't lead to permission and trust."

When I work with clients to transition them from expert to Influencer, they often say: "I'm too uncomfortable to sell. I feel like I'm not a salesperson and I have to continually 'hustle'."

I don't want you to hustle. I want you to sell. And selling is about solving people's problems. We need to replace the word "hustle" with "help". By keeping the word "help" at the front of your mind when engaging in direct contact with clients and leads, you can focus on the problems that need to be solved – not the hard sell. Focusing on solutions will naturally foster a greater sense of trust.

Let's look at the three activities related to the Direct Contact quadrant:

- Database & Newsletter Management
- Daily Visibility
- Phone/Email

DATABASE & NEWSLETTER MANAGEMENT

A client database is an invaluable tool for your business and your brand. Essentially, a database is a store of information about your clients and leads. It helps you convert leads into clients, generates repeat business and helps you build trust and loyalty.

US sales guru Harvey Mackay is an expert on capturing information about clients. He knows everything about his own clients, from their children's names, to their favourite football team, to the date of their wedding anniversary. He developed the "Mackay 66"– a 66-question customer profile that intentionally does not include any information about the products the customer buys. Mackay says we must understand what our clients are like as human beings, rather than consumers, so we can establish relationships, build loyalty, provide extraordinary service and avoid being undercut on prices.

A database can store a wealth of information about your clients and leads, such as:

- Contact information
- Preferred method of contact
- Job title and name of company
- Social media profiles
- Buying history

- Source of lead or how the customer heard about you
- Customer comments
- Special needs

There are countless platforms available to build your database, from a simple Microsoft Excel spreadsheet to customisable database software and online programs. Increasingly, businesses and entrepreneurs are using email marketing platforms such as MailChimp to store their client information.

BUILDING AND MAINTAINING YOUR DATABASE

Being systematic and organised with data input is key to any successful client database. If you don't stay on top of your data input, leads can fall through the cracks and you can lose clients. It's important you build your list right from the word go. Use every opportunity to fill it with leads – people you've met at speaking events, previous clients and people who have contacted you through your website.

According to inbound marketing company HubSpot, your email marketing database degrades by about 22.5% every year.[2] People may opt out of your e-newsletters or change email addresses, so it's important that you not only add fresh contacts to your database constantly, but that you keep your e-newsletter content fresh as well.

If you are building a client database from scratch, or your current one is a little light, fill it with people you already know. This will increase your chances of turning leads into customers. These can be people you know well, such as friends and family, or they can be acquaintances. The idea is not to hassle the people you know, but let them know you are there to help when they need it. Try putting the shoe on the other foot – if you needed help with something, wouldn't you want to work with someone you already have a connection with rather than a stranger?

Networking events are a fantastic way of building your client database. Remember to bring – and swap – your business cards. I don't suggest handing them out to everyone you meet; rather, offer them to people you have a meaningful conversation with and genuinely feel would benefit from what you offer. Make sure you get their business cards and add them to your database as soon as possible. Don't let them languish at the bottom of your bag or briefcase!

---

[2] "25 Simple Ways to Grow Your Email List." HubSpot, March 13, 2015, http://blog.hubspot.com/blog/tabid/6307/bid/32028/25-Clever-Ways-to-Grow-Your-Email-Marketing-List.aspx#sm.0001mt00m4myrcr5zso25xv9zvz4i

CHAPTER 5.1

Lastly, update your database records as changes occur. Regularly back up your database so you don't lose all the priceless information you have gathered. If you have staff, ensure they are trained in how to use the database system.

E-NEWSLETTER LISTS

A client database allows you to tailor marketing campaigns for your audience, and one of the most effective marketing tools is the e-newsletter. An e-newsletter will add leads to your database, explode your conversion rate and foster effective relationships with existing customers.

Research by the Direct Marketing Association found that 66% of online consumers made a purchase because of an email marketing message.[3] So it's no surprise that 89% of marketers say email is their preferred channel for lead generation.[4]

There are countless email marketing platforms available – MailChimp, Active Campaign, AWeber, iContact and Constant Contact, to name a few. Prices vary, but you can often use them for free up to a certain number of subscribers.

So how can you grow your email database? Here are three simple yet effective options:

1. **Your website.** Include an e-newsletter sign-up form on the home page and main pages of your website. Offer an incentive, such as a free e-book, if they sign up. Use your blog to encourage people to sign up for more content via email.

2. **Social media.** Share a sign-up link on your social media platforms and post your latest e-newsletter. Promote a free offer on your Facebook page that requires people to submit their email address.

3. **Events and meet ups.** Any time you attend or speak at an event, ask for the business cards of the people you talk to. Add their details to your email list.

When creating sign-up forms, include required fields so users don't skip vital information, eg. name and email address. Ensure clients have access to their online subscription record so they can update their details as necessary.

---

3 "Saturday Stat Series: The Influence of Email Marketing Messages." Direct Marketing Association, August 3, 2013, https://thedma.org/blog/data-driven-marketing/saturday-stat-series/
4 "Statistics that Prove Email Marketing is (Still) Not Dead." Capterra, February 4, 2016, http://blog.capterra.com/statistics-email-marketing-not-dead/

SPLIT YOUR DATABASE

I recently worked with David, a parenting expert. Parents comprised a large component of his database, which was perfectly logical. The issue was that this market typically had a lower budget. They weren't prepared to pay him thousands of dollars for an engagement – the kind of fee an Influencer would normally command. To turn this around, he needed to take his expertise about relationships to a different market: sales teams. But he couldn't just send out a blanket email to parents *and* sales teams. He needed to create two completely different databases.

Not all clients and leads are the same. They have different backgrounds, problems and needs. You can't pigeonhole them all into the one category. For your e-newsletters to be targeted, relevant and effective, you must split your database.

Your marketing and e-newsletter content needs to be strategic. Sometimes the content you want to share is relevant to all subscribers, but often it's not. For example, if you are a keynote speaker, your subscriber list may include event managers. You may also work with CEOs, HR managers and small business leaders. If you send a global e-newsletter with content that's only relevant to event managers, your message will largely fall on deaf ears. It may even confuse your audience and they may unsubscribe.

Split your database according to your customers' needs and demographics. For example, if you want to promote your message about leadership, you can send an e-newsletter to event managers with a call to action to download your speaker reel. You can then send another e-newsletter to HR managers and senior managers with a link to your leadership white paper. You can send a third email to small business leaders with a link to a brochure that details your leadership training program.

You can still send one e-newsletter to all your subscribers if you wish. But splitting up your database gives you the added option of strategically targeting content to your specific clients, giving you more cut through. Remember, your clients don't sign up to your newsletter – they sign up to you.

PLAN YOUR CONTENT

Content marketing is the creation and distribution of valuable, relevant and consistent content to a clearly defined audience. The aim is to engage your leads and nudge them to the next stage of the buying process.

To remain visible to your audience and gain their trust, your content-rich e-newsletters must be sent regularly. Consistency is key. Decide on how often you're going to send your e-newsletter – fortnightly, weekly or more. Decide what day of the week and the time you will send it, and stick to your schedule. You want your audience to be able to depend on seeing your email land in their inbox. It shows that you are reliable. Even if they don't open every e-newsletter you send, receiving it serves as a regular reminder that you're available when they need you.

Create a content plan. You can plan one month, six months or even 12 months in advance. This ensures you don't run out of ideas. It also keeps the information you share via all your channels of communication (including social media, which we will cover later in this book) consistent.

The ideal content ratio is 80:20. That is, 80% of the content you share should be curated. This means sharing what other experts have said about your subject. Content curation demonstrates to your audience that you genuinely want to assist and educate them.

The remaining 20% should be your own original content with a call to action. Limiting your own content to 20% will help you avoid appearing "salesy". You will be able to highlight your services and offerings without making your audience feel as though they're being sold to. When creating content, think about what you're trying to achieve. What do you want to be known for? Ensure your content is consistent with your message to keep your audience engaged and avoid confusion.

DAILY VISIBILITY

One of my clients, Anne, is a productivity expert. Part of her message is that in this day and age, we can work almost anywhere in the world. Each day, she shares where she is working with her followers on Facebook. Some days, she is on her back deck at her home outside Melbourne, looking out over her pool and having a cup of tea. Other days, she's in New York or China. Seeing her face each day helps me to connect with her at a personal level. She doesn't try to sell to me or share her thought leadership every day, but she brings me into a part of her world so we stay connected. It ensures she's memorable and keeps her front of mind. This means that when someone asks me if I know a productivity expert, I immediately think of Anne.

Customer engagement is so important, and social media offers the perfect opportunity for you to stay connected. In the 12 months prior to August 2015, the number of social media users had risen by 176 million.[5] Yet only 20 Fortune

---

5 "Global Digital Snapshot: August 2015." We Are Social, August 3, 2015, http://wearesocial.com/uk/special-reports/global-statshot-august-2015

500 companies engage with their customers on Facebook.⁶ This goes to show that large companies are underestimating the power of social media. And one of the most influential platforms is Instagram. In fact, in more than 475 global campaigns, Nielsen found that ad recall on Instagram exceeded Nielsen's norms for online advertising by almost three times.⁷

So what does all this mean? Most customers hang out on social media. It pays to research the demographics of your ideal customer and identify what social media platforms they use. You may think your clients check in more often on Facebook, but they may actually hang out on LinkedIn.

By making yourself visible on your clients' social networks every day, the easier you make it for them to trust you and the more likely they'll recommend you others. The goal is to ensure your customer sees your face (your profile photo) and message consistently to create a strong sense of familiarity and recall when they need help.

My experience working with industry leaders is that the ones with the most powerful positioning hang out and focus on three different social media platforms. Keep in mind that different industries hang out on different platforms. For example, in 2015, a Macquarie Group Benchmarking report found a correlation between mortgage brokers with profiles on LinkedIn, Facebook and Twitter and high-performing mortgage brokering practices.⁸ So, if you're currently only using one platform, increase your chances of success by adding two others to your social-media arsenal. Think of it as "ring-fencing" – a term mortgage brokers use for selling more than one loan product to a client. Ensure you ring-fence your clients across all your communication channels – social media, e-newsletters and offline activities, too. It takes 10 pieces of content for someone to decide to work with you, and social networks are one of the most effective ways to get that content in front of your audience quickly.

You need to work on your visibility every day – not once a week or whenever you remember. Without daily visibility, your positioning as an Influencer is compromised. People will forget who you are. If they have an issue you can solve, you must remain front of mind by making your presence known day in, day out.

---

6 "Marketing: 96 Amazing Social Media Statistics and Facts." Brandwatch, March 7, 2016, https://www.brandwatch.com/blog/96-amazing-social-media-statistics-and-facts-for-2016/
7 "The Next Steps for Ads on Instagram: New Formats, Increased Relevance, Broader Availability." Instagram, http://blog.business.instagram.com/post/120537653811/the-next-steps-for-ads-on-instagram-new-formats
8 "Building sustainable success: 2015 Mortgage Broking Benchmarking Report." Macquarie, https://www.macquarie.com/dafiles/Internet/mgl/global/advisers/docs/campaigns/2015-mortgages-benchmarking-report.pdf?v=2

CHAPTER 5.1

PHONE/EMAIL CALL CYCLES (OR OTHER COOL WAYS TO DO THIS!)

Email is the Jason Bourne of the internet. Someone is always trying to kill him but he just won't die!

There's no doubt that email is essential to keeping the channels of communication open with clients. It's intimate and one on one. Think of it as having a virtual coffee with your client. But don't forget the power of a simple phone call.

In business, the phone is being used less and less. You may worry that you're bothering people by calling them. It also takes more effort. Email seems to be the safer option. Yet, although email can be an efficient way of communicating, it can lack that personal touch needed to create a strong connection with your client.

Overly relying on emails to communicate can create an emotional distance. Emails lack the subtle nuances of audible speech; the pauses, emphasis and subtle feeling that help us to understand each other clearly. It's easier to misinterpret the tone of voice in a slab of text than it is when listening to someone speak. In a phone call, you can't hide behind your computer; you have no choice but to be more attentive, empathetic and personable. All things that help build trust and your positioning as an Influencer.

Furthermore, it's easy for clients and leads to ignore an email. But if you call them, it's much easier to engage with them, have a meaningful conversation and get things moving. Be brave, take the initiative and pick up the phone. You will open yourself up to more opportunities.

The secret to making this work is twofold. Firstly, have time allocated in your calendar each day to reach out. You might need 30-45 minutes if you're working on your own; less if you are delegating to an assistant. Secondly, you need to make a list the night before of five people you could contact the following day. This way, you won't procrastinate when it's time to pick up the phone and reach out.

In our hectic, disconnected worlds, people are touched by the little things. Check in on your clients regularly. Find out what they're up to, what they're working on and if they need assistance with anything. Your interest and desire to help won't go unnoticed. Remember, current clients are a valuable source of referrals. If you can show them you are genuinely interested in them by staying connected, they are more likely to refer you to others.

It's also often the case that a client has been meaning to contact you, but they have been so busy dealing with the chaos of their daily lives that they simply haven't been able to. If you are the one to reach out first, they'll be more likely to engage your services.

Think of creative ways you can do this!

CASE STUDY

**LACHIE PENNEFATHER:
CEO OF STREAKA VIDEO**

1. You have a cool product called Streaka. Tell us how it works.

Streaka Video evolved from the need for a short-form branded video solution that could be adopted into anyone's business framework. We had mobile and branding in mind, so we came from the angle that this needed to be video for communication and relationship building – done on the fly, no editing, just do! Why not give the people you do business with and those who are interested in your business some one-to-one personal customer service? The idea is that when you do this continually, the aggregate positive effect on your business is profound. Empower your customers to share their experience with you to their networks. This cements existing business and, importantly, brings in new leads.

In addition, we were after a solution that would allow us to easily introduce the medium of video to a business and have it up and running in a very short time. People traditionally associate video with high-end production, big costs and lots of time. We came from an approach of, "Let's use video to talk to customers in bite-size pieces," as this is how we consume information today.

The following points were key to the process of how it works:

- Videos had to be done from a smartphone: simply record, name the video and submit.
- It had to be fast with simple options to save, delete and share.
- The user did not have to know anything about technology or editing suites. They simply recorded and out the other end, due to automation, came a video that had been imprinted with their personal or business brand. Thus, they could empower everyone in their business to use video.

- The recipient of the video watches it on the business's branded pages, which may have calls to action to encourage the recipient to do something further.

2. Why is it so powerful?

Human nature dictates that when you give someone personal time, good information and content of value, you will be rewarded for your efforts. They will talk about you, recommend you and you will get referral business.

We adapt this to the way we use Streaka Video. It's powerful in that it's simple to use but, most importantly, you can be very specific and personal with the content you make. You can send many videos out to people and very quickly address their particular scenario, whether you are answering a question, keeping them informed or introducing yourself to a potential customer. One is only limited by one's actions. The fact we are a branded video solution also adds weight to "you" the brand.

The real power lies in the effect your video communication has on your recipients. People simply like to receive a video, and when it's personal to them and you answer their questions or acknowledge their interaction, say no more. Let the powers that be do their thing. You have done your part, let others tell others about you. Simple.

3. What type of experts do you see using this technology?

People are busy in general and don't have the resources or time for the production of marketing, promotion and communication material. They just need to be conducting their daily business, making sales and getting new business. Their brand is extremely important to them as well.

We have experts from all sorts of different fields: financial advisers, real estate agents, speakers, law firms, physiotherapists, support staff for software services, personal trainers, travel agents. They all have clients they need to keep informed. There is no day that goes by where there isn't a reason to get in touch with existing clients.

A common thread amongst our users – and this is from feedback – is that with the advent of social media, we often lose sight of those we already do business with. They see that being able to give a personalised communication service to existing customers automatically drives new leads and referrals. You just about close the lead before you even get it because you place great value on one-to-one customer service for existing clients.

4. Can you give us an example of how it has helped an expert in their field generate leads?

I would like to share a story of one of our best users, a financial adviser from Newcastle. Let's name him John.

John explained to us that one of the greatest problems with his business and industry was simply keeping people informed. It was a challenge to keep them up to date on how their investments were performing and new opportunities. Weeks and months would slip by.

John now sets himself a daily *minimum* KPI of five videos to be sent out before he does anything that day. This takes 10 minutes. He does them on the fly wherever he is. It's simply about communicating and keeping people informed. As he said to me, "I don't even know if they listen to what I say, it's the fact that I contact them – that's what they appreciate. It takes me two minutes to do each video."

John has been doing this for nearly a year. His face and brand go out with every video. Wherever it is viewed, it's on his branded business page. He says he receives consistent referrals from his existing customer base because he is seen as a good communicator. He keeps his videos short, informal and to the point, and keeps it real. As he says, "Many of my clients expect a video from me. They actually enjoy the updates and so I make the point of keeping the content light, fun and personable. I build real trust with them."

For us at Streaka Video, we get a lot of referral business because of John. Other advisers see what he does and they speak amongst themselves.

Scan to see a sample:

CHAPTER 5.1

FOLLOWING UP

You've probably heard the phrase, "the fortune is in the follow-up". John Maxwell, American expert in leadership, says: "Diligent follow-up and follow-through will set you apart form the crowd and communicate excellence."

In his landmark book, *Influence: The Psychology of Persuasion*, Robert Cialdini says it typically takes five to seven touch points for someone to change their behaviour, or for you to get them to do something. When working with sales teams, Cialdini found about 80% of prospects convert after the fifth to seventh contact. The problem is that we give up easily because we don't want to be annoying.

Following up with leads and clients seems an obvious part of running a business, yet it's amazing how few people do. Following up via phone or email is simple and effective, as long as it comes from a place of help rather than hustle. As Jill Konrath, expert in business-to-business selling, says: "You have to drop your sales mentality and start working with your prospects as if they've already hired you."

So, take the time to set reminders for follow-up calls for all your proposals. All it takes is that little bit of extra effort on your part and your conversions will skyrocket.

SET GUIDELINES AND EXPECTATIONS

I remember chatting with Karen, one of my clients and a leadership expert, who told me that she had missed out on a keynote speaking event because she took 40 minutes to respond to the event planner. They needed someone quickly and Karen missed out. She realised she needed to have a more responsive system in place for her sales. One of the KPIs we set in her business – and one I set for many Influencers – is a sales response time of eight minutes. Each sales response time is recorded so we can improve the times, and we celebrate when we get under eight minutes.

The value of being able to respond quickly cannot be underestimated. Recently, I interviewed certified meeting professional Deborah Gardner on my podcast, the Jane Anderson Show. Gardner is one of the most booked speakers in the US. She attributes her in-demand booking schedule to her responsiveness. She says that meeting planners will always choose a speaker who is easy to work with and responsive over a rock star.

Ensure you are responsive by setting timeframes for returning phone calls and emails. Clients and leads get irritated when their queries go unanswered.

However, you also need to set boundaries. You don't want to be "on call" day and night. Decide on what is a reasonable time for you to respond to queries. Set guidelines for yourself and stick to them as much as you can. Is it reasonable for your clients and leads to wait 24 hours for a response? Or are eight hours more appropriate? Or five minutes?

You may need to invest in some online calendar scheduling tools, virtual assistant support, templates, brochures, web copy and systemised procedures to reduce the amount of time wasted and increase response times.

LEARN TO SAY NO

A can-do attitude is a wonderful asset for an Influencer, but equally as important is the ability to say "no".

Saying no isn't easy. When we're building a business, we often say yes to everything. We shy away from saying no because we don't want to offend. We worry that saying no will burn our bridges with our clients.

But the more you say no, the more trust you build. Bluffing your way through gaps of knowledge or a lack of skills is an invitation for disaster. If a client contacts you via phone or email asking for something but you truly cannot help them, let them know. They will appreciate your honesty. Even better, refer them to someone who can help them. This will enhance your trustworthiness and dependability.

As Steve Jobs said, "It's only by saying 'no' that you can concentrate on the things that are really important."

CHAPTER 5.1

QUESTIONS FOR YOU TO CONSIDER:

1. On a scale of 1 to 10, how much love would your clients say you show them?

___

2. On a scale of 1 to 10, how much love do you think you show them?

___

3. What platform do you use for your client database (or CRM)? For example, MailChimp or Active Campaign.

___

4. Do you know what is important to your clients in their careers and lives? Have you captured this in your CRM?

___

5. How much time have you allocated each week to build, manage and maintain your database? (Hint: Even just 30 minutes per week can be all you need to ensure it is well-looked after!)

___

6. What different lists have you split your e-newsletter database into? Do they reflect your different buyers?

___

7. What day have you scheduled to send out your e-newsletter?

_____
_____

8. What content do you plan to write for the next 3-6 months for each of those newsletters?

_____
_____
_____

9. How do you plan to stay visible to your social audience each day? (Hint: Cat videos are not the right answer!)

_____
_____
_____

10. How many clients do you plan to call this week? How many will you email?

_____
_____
_____

11. What will you say to them when you reach out? Write your script.

_____
_____
_____

12. List 10 clients you can contact this week to share what you're doing and find out if they need your help.

_____
_____
_____

13. What time have you set as your KPI for returning calls and emails from prospective clients?

_____
_____

CHAPTER 5.1

14. Which clients do you need to follow up?

_____
_____
_____

15. When will you follow them up?

_____
_____
_____

16. What will you say?

_____
_____
_____

17. What KPIs do you have in place for clients you need to follow up in the future?

_____
_____

18. How will you ensure they're followed? For example, reminders in your CRM or calendar.

_____
_____

19. What events have you got coming up that you could create a video for to introduce yourself?

_____
_____
_____

20. Look at your calendar for the next month. What appointments have you already scheduled? What is missing? Are there appointments you need to say no to or delegate? When will you follow them up?

_____
_____

CHAPTER 5.2

Network or Search

"Make your product easier to buy than your competition, or you will find your customers buying from them, not you."
– Mark Cuban

Strong networks combined with an effective online search strategy create a powerful selling force. Networks are a pot of gold: a prized source of inbound referrals, repeat business and recommendations. Yet you also need to be easily found by people outside your networks. Search engine visibility attracts more leads, clinches sales and solidifies your positioning as an Influencer.

Referrals are the lifeblood of sales. People are much more willing to work with someone endorsed by their own networks. If someone they trust recommends you, the potential client is much more likely to get in touch with you. It's a cost-effective, organic way for you to expand your network.

However, you cannot rely on referrals alone. Often, people will still want to find out as much information about you as they can before they decide to contact you. An online search will give them the facts and reassurances they need, so it's vital you turn up in search results.

Online searches are also crucial for appealing to clients who have no idea you exist. If someone outside your networks is looking for a service you can provide, it's essential that your website and social media profiles are search engine optimised. This ensures you appear in the search results – preferably on page one.

So, you cannot rely on your networks alone to elevate your positioning as an Influencer. You must take a two-pronged approach to generating leads by optimising your website and online search results as well.

The three activities related to the Network or Search quadrant are:

- LinkedIn SEO
- Google Search/SEO/AdWords
- Networks (Referrals)

CHAPTER 5.2

LINKEDIN SEO

Did you know that two LinkedIn accounts are created every second? By the end of 2016, there were more than 450 million members[1] and it's not running out of steam any time soon! LinkedIn presents an enormous opportunity for you to grow your networks and skyrocket your leads.

One of the reasons why LinkedIn is so popular is that it has no direct competition. And it plans to keep it that way. LinkedIn is staying ahead of the game through strategic mergers and acquisitions. In 2013, LinkedIn acquired professional content sharing platform SlideShare. Two years later, in 2015, it acquired leading online education company Lynda.com for $1.5 billion. This is known as vertical integration: adding related services that create a better user experience.

With more than 467 million LinkedIn users around the world, it's safe to say it's working.

WHAT EXACTLY IS LINKEDIN?

LinkedIn is a social networking site for businesses and professionals. It was created in 2003 and is one of the most advanced and complex social media platforms in existence. LinkedIn enables you to engage with and influence your peers, clients and potential customers. Originally created for executives, LinkedIn has grown to connect professionals at all levels. It is available in 24 languages and has members listed in more than 200 countries. It's had a dramatic impact on the way business is done and has been a game changer for companies, professionals and entrepreneurs.

First and foremost, LinkedIn is a search engine. It allows users to search for people, companies, job titles and more. It acts like Google, so having the right keywords in your profile is critical to turning up in search results. And not only will you turn up in LinkedIn search results, you're more likely to turn up in a Google search, too. The advantage of this is that you have more opportunity to be found by your target audience and grow your networks.

SEARCH ENGINE OPTIMISE YOUR PROFILE

To be search engine optimised, your profile must contain the keywords that will get you seen in search results. Keywords are the words and phrases people type into online search engines – such as Google, Bing and Yahoo – to find businesses and people like you.

---

1 "Number of LinkedIn members from 1st quarter 2009 to 3rd quarter 2016 (in millions)." Statista, https://www.statista.com/statistics/274050/quarterly-numbers-of-linkedin-members/

There are three key factors to ensuring your LinkedIn profile has excellent SEO keywords:

1. **Relevance.** Use the words and phrases your potential clients would use when searching for you. For example, if you're a Sydney-based leadership keynote speaker, a customer needing your services might type "leadership speaker Sydney" into the LinkedIn search field. Someone else might type "leadership keynote speaker" or "leadership trainer Sydney". Having these keywords strategically placed in your profile means people will find you for what you want to be found for.

2. **Competitiveness.** Some keywords are more competitive than others. To get a strong, targeted result, be specific. For example, the keyword "coach" is a competitive keyword. There are plenty of coaches in all kinds of industries. On its own, "coach" is too general – it doesn't specify what you do. But if you change the keyword to "executive coach", you will get a better search result.

3. **Location.** The location of your keywords is also important. You don't want your profile to read like spam; the keywords need to be strategically placed so your content has a natural flow. For maximum SEO, you also need to include keywords in the following five areas of your profile: headline, summary, employment history, skills and endorsements, and recommendations.

A significant advantage of having a search engine optimised LinkedIn profile is that it's generally cheaper than hiring an SEO expert to optimise your website. So, considering this, let's expand on the five areas of your LinkedIn profile that significantly impact your SEO:

1. **Title.** You have 120 characters to work with in your title.
   It must contain your keywords and reflect the problems
   you solve. A well-written title distinguishes you from people with similar skills, giving you more cut through with your audience.

2. **Summary.** This is the most viewed section on LinkedIn. It is an encapsulation of you and your brand. It allows you to explain what you do, who you help and how you help. Your summary positions you to reach your target audience, validates you and allows you to create a strong call to action.

3. **Employment History.** I often see clients treat their employment history section like an obituary of their past jobs. Despite the word "history", this section should be focused on the future. You have up to 2000 characters

to illustrate each position you have held. Remember, you are writing for your audience, not for you. Make sure your employment history reflects your clients' problems. Engage them by demonstrating how the roles you've had can help you solve their problems.

4. **Skills and Endorsements.** This section allows your LinkedIn connections to validate your strengths and expertise. Skills and endorsements paint an immediate picture of your abilities. You might be surprised to see that people have endorsed you for skills you've never had, yet this section carries a heavy weighting in the search results. The good news is, you can take control of them. You can manually add skills and expertise to your profile so they reflect your business goals. You also don't have to accept what others endorse you for. LinkedIn gives you the capacity to include up to 50 skills, but I suggest taking the "less is more" route. It's far more effective to have 10 strong skills on your profile than 50 weak ones.

5. **Recommendations.** You need to place a high priority on this section. Recommendations are a form of "social proof". When someone is looking at working with you, they need to see that others have verified you as great to work with. It creates that all-important sense of trust and elevates your positioning. If you are a little light on recommendations, you can offer to help your connections write one for you. Be sure to write one for them in return.

REMEMBER TO REACH OUT

Don't make the mistake of creating your LinkedIn profile, sitting back and waiting for people to connect with you. As is the case in the offline world, clients and leads don't magically appear on LinkedIn. You need to push things along. As US basketballer Michael Jordan said, "Some people want it to happen, some wish it would happen, others make it happen."

Take control of your LinkedIn network. Search for people you want to connect with. Personalise your connection requests and make it a humanised experience. A great way to expand your network is by joining LinkedIn groups related to your industry and areas of expertise. Share your comments and insights with the group, and start conversations. You'll get noticed and people will want to connect with you. (We'll take a more in-depth look at how you can proactively make connections on LinkedIn in Chapter 5.3 – Awareness.)

And don't forget to make it easy for others to connect with you. Respond to requests to connect in a timely manner, and remember to share your LinkedIn profile link on your website, promotional material and other social media platforms.

GOOGLE SEARCH/SEO/ADWORDS

"The best place to hide a dead body is page two of Google Search results."
– Unknown

Google is the most-used online search engine in the world. It handles billions of searches every day. As an Influencer, the power you can wield through effective Google SEO is phenomenal.

Between 80%-90% of customers check online reviews prior to making a purchase.[2] These online reviews are largely found by conducting a Google search. In addition, the 2014 State of B2B procurement study from Acquity Group found that 94% of business buyers do some form of research online – and 77% of these buyers use a Google search.[3] So, by reaching more people through Google, you can quickly add to your client database and build your networks.

GOOGLE ADWORDS

Google AdWords is a paid advertising service. It allows you to place brief ads alongside Google search results at the top or side of the results screen. The idea is that people will notice your business when they do a Google search for a service like yours. You only pay for your ad whenever someone clicks on it. This is known as cost-per-click advertising (CPC).

AdWords allows you to target your ideal clients across multiple platforms – computers, tablets and mobile phones. You can customise your ads based on your goals by including a clickable button that takes clients to your website or store. You can even prompt them to call your business or install an app. By carefully selecting your keywords, you can target your ads to people who are searching for related terms. You can also choose to advertise at a certain time of day.

To find out what keywords will increase your searchability, check out Google AdWords' Keyword Planner. This is a free tool that generates keyword ideas and estimates how they will perform in Google searches. To access Google Keyword Planner, you need to set up an AdWords account. Visit https://adwords.google.com/KeywordPlanner

---

2 "7 Reasons Why Your Business Should Invest in SEO." *Forbes*, March 26, 2014, http://www.forbes.com/sites/steveolenski/2014/03/26/7-reasons-why-your-business-should-invest-in-seo/#2af558551337
3 "94 percent of B2B buyers research online for purchase decisions." Brafton, October 28, 2014, http://www.brafton.com/news/94-percent-b2b-buyers-research-online-purchase-decisions/

CHAPTER 5.2

NETWORKS (REFERRALS)

> *"People influence people. Nothing influences people more than a recommendation from a trusted friend. A trusted referral influences people more than the best broadcast message. A trusted referral is the holy grail of advertising."*
> *– Mark Zuckerberg*

Your networks provide you with your most powerful sales source: inbound referrals. About one half of my own business comes from inbound referrals. Every client you have and every person you meet has the potential to connect you with dozens of leads.

But your contacts won't send referrals your way unless you deserve them. You must earn referrals by building positive relationships with everyone you meet.

When someone has a problem, one of the first things they do is ask their networks for advice on who can help them. If their networks positively endorse you as the right person for the job, the potential client is more likely to want to work with you as they feel reassured. People are much more comfortable working with someone they know, or with someone their friends know, than a person they know nothing about.

RETURN THE FAVOUR

Whenever you can, return the favour. In business, there is a lot of truth in the adage, "You scratch my back, I'll scratch yours." By giving referrals generously yourself, others will be more motivated to share referrals with you. You will be top of mind when they come across your ideal client.

And remember to be courteous. Always thank someone who has given you a referral. If you fail to acknowledge their generosity, they'll be less inclined to refer you to others in the future.

GIFT GIVING

> *"The real currency of networking is not greed, but generosity."*
> *– Keith Ferrazzi*

Give and you shall receive! Gift giving is a wonderful way to establish respectful, positive relationships with people in your networks. Which, of course, leads to more referrals and greater positioning.

But gift giving must be thoughtful. According to Deb Brown, American expert in gift giving and founder of Touch Your Client's Heart, a gift must:

- **Be meaningful.** Avoid last-minute, generic gifts from large shopping centres. Instead, seek smaller, more personal shops and boutiques that offer unique gifts.

- **Be thoughtful.** Consider the person you're buying for. How have they helped you? Keep this in mind as you search for a present that will help you return the favour.

- **Be memorable.** Give a gift that will be cherished for years to come. Flowers and chocolate have a short shelf life! Buy something special, such as a monogrammed picnic blanket or a book on a subject they're passionate about.

- **Be personable.** Choose something that speaks to the person's unique qualities. If you don't know their likes and dislikes, find out. Not everyone drinks wine or eats truffles. What would they appreciate?

Choosing the right gift for clients and important contacts can be a challenge, but it works wonders for building relationships. For example, I don't drink alcohol. It's not that I'm a recovering alcoholic – I simply choose to not drink as it makes me tired and I feel like it stays in my body for days. But people often give me a bottle of wine as a gift. It's considered a "safe" option for most people, but for me, it's like nails down a chalkboard. I don't take it personally, but when someone does give me a gift they've put some thought into, it shows they care. I feel as though they really know and value me.

Gift giving says a lot about you. Make sure your gift giving is considered and touches the hearts of your important contacts and clients. After all, reaching the hearts of our audiences is what being an Influencer is all about.

INDUSTRY INFLUENCER SPOTLIGHT
DEB BROWN: GIFT-GIVING EXPERT

1. What is it about gift giving that creates the trigger for a referral?

Whatever you put out in the world comes back to you. When someone does something nice for you, you naturally want to return the favour. When referral partners understand that giving you a referral is appreciated because you thank them with a gift, they are more likely to send referrals again.

2. What are the best gifts to buy to achieve referrals?

I recommend giving a thank you gift after the referral. The best gifts for this purpose are consumable in some way. You want your referral partner to enjoy the gift, use it up, then be happy to receive it again when they give another referral. Food, gift cards and flowers all make great consumable gifts.

3. When are the best times to send a gift?

Gifts can be sent immediately after a sale to welcome and thank the new client for investing in your service. They can also be sent at the end of a project to thank the client for doing business with you. You can send annual gifts for ongoing and long-term clients, but choose a time outside traditional holidays to make it stand out. You can also send gifts at random times. Doing that catches people by surprise and makes the gift more memorable.

4. What information should I have in my files about clients?

Depending on your business, you may wish to celebrate client birthdays, anniversaries, their purchase of a new home, or other special dates. To do this, you need to plan ahead and gather the information as part of your on-boarding process. You may also want to learn your clients' hobbies and interests, family make-up and other important details. You want to know what is important to them. As you get to know the details about them, you will be able to customise gifts and conversations to build a relationship that will, in turn, build loyalty.

TESTIMONIALS

Testimonials have amazing selling power. They don't cost you anything (besides providing your clients with first-class service). They have no shelf life: you can use them over and over on different platforms – both online and offline – to build awareness. And they provide potential clients with the reassurance that you can deliver what you say you will.

People are naturally sceptical. They need many questions answered before they decide if they want to work with you. Testimonials create trust because they substantiate your claims without being salesy. They are unbiased and genuine, and are evidence of how you can make a real difference to people's lives.

Testimonials work wonders for your target audience because:

1. **They give hope.** Reading or hearing a glowing endorsement makes people think, "Wow, I would love for that to happen for me!" They connect the dots between what you've done for others and what you can do for them, without you having to spell it out for them.

2. **What others say about us is more important than what we say about ourselves.** Tone down the self-selling and let others do the talking. It helps build trust.

3. **They leverage your positioning.** Seeing that others endorse you – especially people who are leaders themselves – sends a clear message to potential clients that you are dependable and an expert in your field.

4. **Potential clients see themselves in the people you have helped.** People want to relate to other people. They consciously and subconsciously look for shared characteristics. Potential clients will try to make a connection between themselves and the person giving the testimonial. You want them to think, "They're just like me. That's exactly the problem I'm having." They'll be more likely to have confidence in you and make contact.

5. **It's easy.** Testimonials get straight to the point. They do all the hard work for you. You can save time and energy by replacing a truckload of your own content with carefully selected recommendations and testimonials. This is particularly helpful if you are struggling with a tight word count!

Don't be afraid to ask your clients for testimonials. Keep the request simple by asking for a sentence or two on how you have helped them. This isn't asking for much and usually they will be happy to oblige. Often, they will provide you with more than just a one-sentence answer. And if someone gives you positive feedback in an email, ask them if you can use it as a testimonial.

You can also ask your peers and colleagues for testimonials. If they have worked alongside you, read your blogs or – better yet – read your book, ask them for a brief review. This will cement your credibility as a leader in your field.

A testimonial page on your website is a must. It's one of the first pages a visitor will go to when they land on your website. Maximise the benefits of your testimonials by including them on your home page and in sidebars.

Share your testimonials on your social media platforms, including LinkedIn and Facebook. Not everyone visits your website regularly, so social media allows you to achieve daily visibility with your testimonials. You can also use them to add authenticity to your print advertising by including them in breakout boxes and quotes.

CHOOSE THE RIGHT TESTIMONIALS

For a testimonial to make an impact, it needs to state more than just the facts. It needs to demonstrate the benefits. For example: "Your leadership program was fantastic! I loved it and learnt a lot. Thanks." Sure, this is a nice testimonial, but it doesn't show your audience what your services can do for them. It doesn't pack much of a punch.

You want your testimonials to clearly articulate how you can change people's lives. For example: "After attending your leadership course, I tripled my amount of leads. This led to a 40% increase in sales within three months!" This is a much more effective testimonial. It shows real, quantitative results that everyone wants.

Potential clients need to know that your testimonials are from real people. Ensure your testimonials include first and last names, job title and where the person is from. For example, "John King, CEO, The Leadership Factory, Sydney", is much more credible than simply "John, NSW." Furthermore, make sure your testimonials are from people your clients can relate to. If you're targeting CEOs, then provide testimonials from other CEOs and senior leaders. Your clients will be more responsive to testimonials from their peers.

THINK OUTSIDE THE TEXT BOX

Want to make even more of an impact? Try audio or video testimonials. Events and training sessions present the ideal opportunity to capture these kinds of testimonials. It also requires less effort from the person giving the testimonial.

Audio and visual testimonials add interest to your website, and you can share them on social media and in your e-newsletters.

TRIGGER EVENTS

Trigger events are a fantastic way of increasing referrals. This process involves a trigger event before your sale, and a trigger event after your sale. So, two of the most valuable networks you can build are people who get a sale from your client before you, and a sale from your client after you. It's an often-overlooked part of lead generation, but it is effective.

For example, from time to time, I receive enquiries from people looking to make changes to their careers. This is because I used to be a career practitioner. I'm not a career practitioner anymore, so nowadays, I refer these people to other career practitioners in my network (trigger event before my sale). Sometimes, it's better for my clients to talk to a career practitioner and explore their career options before deciding they want to be an Influencer in a particular industry. So, after they talk to the career practitioner, they often come back to me (my sale) so we can create a strategy that positions them as an Influencer. I then might refer them to a copywriter, who the client then engages to help them write their blogs (trigger event after the sale).

GOAL	TRIGGER EVENT BEFORE	IDEAL CLIENT	TRIGGER EVENT AFTER
To sell more keynotes	Venue managers	Meeting planner	Caterer
To sell more executive career coaching	Resume writer	Executive job seeker	Recruiter

These examples could also work the other way around. For example, the job seeker may have approached the recruiter first. Either way, each trigger event needs to either refer you back or forward.

CHAPTER 5.2

QUESTIONS FOR YOU TO CONSIDER:

1. Which keywords are most relevant for your LinkedIn profile?

_____
_____
_____
_____

2. Where will you put them in your profile to maximise your SEO?

_____
_____
_____
_____

3. Which keywords need to be part of your website SEO?

_____
_____
_____
_____

4. How many connections or referrals have you made in the past week?

_____
_____
_____
_____

5. Have you set a reminder for at least one day in your calendar to do introductions?

_____
_____
_____
_____

6. Where do you capture your clients' likes and dislikes?

_____
_____
_____
_____

7. When you Google your area of expertise and the word "expert" (eg. "marketing expert"), who turns up in the search results?

_____
_____
_____

8. Looking at the Google keyword tool, how much money are people paying for ads to help them appear at the top of search results?

_____
_____
_____

9. How many keyword searches are done each month using your keywords?

_____
_____
_____

10. Which words will you choose for your AdWords advertising campaign? This is not recommended until you have strong positioning in your area of expertise (generally, turning over $500,000 pa).

_____
_____
_____

11. How many pages of your website do you need to search engine optimise? How long will this take you? When will you do it? (Hint: Do one page and record how long it took to complete. Multiply this time by the number of pages you want to optimise, and allocate the time in your calendar.)

_____
_____
_____

12. Which clients will you ask for testimonials?

_____
_____
_____

CHAPTER 5.2

13. Which testimonials will you add to the testimonials page on your website?

_____
_____
_____

14. Where else can you can use your testimonials for maximum effect?

_____
_____
_____

15. Consider your trigger events. What is the sale after you and what is the sale before you?

_____
_____
_____

16. How long will it take you to reach out to those trigger event referrers? Allocate time in your calendar to reach out to these people and offer to connect with them.

_____
_____
_____

17. What gifts best support your message when working with clients?

_____
_____
_____

18. Who are your top 25 clients?

_____
_____
_____
_____
_____

19. What habits and routines do you need to set up to nurture them?

_____
_____
_____

20. What is your communication plan to keep in touch with them?

_____
_____
_____

CHAPTER 5.2

CHAPTER 5.3

Awareness

"Awareness is the greatest agent for change."
– Eckhart Tolle

Have you ever been on a date and things moved too fast, too soon? Within an hour or two, you knew your date's life story and they were ready to pack their bags and move in with you. Or perhaps things didn't move quickly enough? It was too hard to get to know the person and you lost interest entirely.

Creating an awareness of your personal brand is a lot like dating. You need to let your audience get to know you. They need to know who you are before they can trust you. Understanding what you do, who you help and where you're coming from is critical. Otherwise, they won't see you as the genuine, credible and dependable person you are. They'll lose interest, disconnect and look for someone else to help them.

Awareness is the first step towards customer loyalty. According to PMR Research's Brand Awareness and Customer Loyalty research paper, "Within a set of familiar brands, consumers pick the ones better known to them especially if they cannot see any special differences between competing offerings."[1] Furthermore, "brand recall coupled with high customer satisfaction levels translate into customer loyalty."

Awareness is the first step towards familiarity, and familiarity creates trust. Put yourself in the shoes of your potential clients. Working with someone new is a risk. You present unfamiliar territory: their money, time and reputation are at stake. But if you can become familiar to them by creating an awareness of who you are and what you do, their perceived amount of risk decreases significantly. They will feel comfortable and have more confidence working with you.

Be proactive about creating awareness. Don't sit back and wait for people to come to you and ask questions. Take the initiative and reach out to them. Start the conversations – online and offline.

---

[1] "Brand Awareness and Customer Loyalty." PMR Research, February 2012, http://www.research-pmr.com/userfiles/file/wp/Brand-Awareness-and-Customer-Loyalty.pdf

CHAPTER 5.3

Take a genuine interest in your audience and you'll become not just visible, but memorable. People will be more likely to want to work with you. Better yet, they'll be singing you praises with recommendations and testimonials, which will boost your reputation and credibility even further.

The three activities related to the Awareness quadrant are:

- Proactive Connections
- Referrals
- Speak

PROACTIVE CONNECTIONS

"If you're proactive, you don't have to wait for circumstances or other people to create perspective-expanding experiences. You can consciously create your own."
- Dr Stephen Covey

Having the right connections can make or break your positioning as an Influencer. You not only need solid networks to build an awareness of what you do and generate leads; you need a supportive network of people you can depend on when things don't go to plan.

But meeting people doesn't just happen. This is especially true when so much of our business lives are conducted online. If you don't actively pursue opportunities to connect, you won't grow your networks. At least, not with the kinds of people you want to surround yourself with. Your leads will run dry. Your practice will stagnate. You'll feel frustrated and lose confidence in yourself as an Influencer.

You may be hesitant to proactively connect with others because you don't know how. You may feel as though you don't know what to say or how to start the conversation. You may worry you'll appear pushy or that people will be suspicious of your intentions, thinking all you want is to make a quick sale. In reality, most people will be touched that you've reached out to them. The fact you've taken the time and made the effort to connect won't go unnoticed.

The first thing to do when approaching someone is to look for common ground. It makes things easier for you both. What mutual interests do you have? How are you alike? What do you know about the person? Find out as much as you can about them and ask plenty of questions. Show them you're interested. It can be daunting at first, but the more you put yourself out there, the more confident you'll become.

Influencers connect proactively in a super-efficient way. They're highly leveraged, focus on the best use of their time and connect at the *right* time. In *Sell Your Thoughts*, Matt Church discusses the focus on becoming a representative of chapter committees, such as the International Coach Federation or National Speakers Association. However, if you are early in your journey, this is not a great strategic move. It's better done at a higher level, when you're earning $500,000 per year or more. Early in your career, you can waste a lot of time when your focus should be on selling.

However, there are proactive activities you can engage in regardless of the level your business is at. Ideally, these activities should be part of your routine. These include LinkedIn connections, speaking and referrals.

LINKEDIN CONNECTIONS

One of the most common complaints I hear from people about LinkedIn is: "I don't get anything from it." Yet, when I ask them about the number of ideal clients they have tried to reach out to LinkedIn, the response it typically "none". The reality is that only 10% of the opportunities available to you on LinkedIn will come to you. About 90% will happen because you have reached out and made them happen. You need to put the effort in.

LinkedIn presents a fantastic opportunity to connect with your peers and potential clients. Once you're connected, their awareness and understanding of you will be a natural progression – provided you use LinkedIn regularly and strategically.

You can quickly build your LinkedIn network by connecting with:

- Colleagues
- Past colleagues
- Clients
- People from networking events
- Industry leaders
- Experts in your field
- Fellow students from classes or workshops you have attended

To send a connection request, simply search for the person you want to connect with, then click on "Connect" underneath their title. You can also click on the "Grow My Network" icon in the top right-hand corner of your screen to see a list of people you may know.

CHAPTER 5.3

KEEP IT PERSONAL

It seems simple, yet most people fail to personalise their LinkedIn connection requests. Nobody likes to feel as though they are "just another number" – yet by keeping your requests dull and detached, that's exactly the message you send.

LinkedIn's default message is: "I'd like to add you to my professional network on LinkedIn." Not exactly engaging, is it? Personalise it by adding extra detail. It demonstrates that you've done your research and genuinely want to get to know the person. For example, "Hi John. It was great to meet you at the conference last week. I thoroughly enjoyed your presentation. Thanks so much for sharing your expertise."

Keep in mind that you can only send personalised requests from the desktop version of LinkedIn. You don't have the option on your tablet or mobile phone.

LET YOUR CONNECTIONS GET TO KNOW YOU

The next step in the connection process is to maintain your visibility. You want your new connections to get to know you so they can trust you. Think of it like dating: you don't want to come on too strong, but you need to let your personality and attributes shine.

Educate your audience by feeding them regular bits of information. Explain what you do and how you can help them. Offer your insights. You can do this by posting regularly on LinkedIn and your other social media accounts, writing and sharing your blogs, and commenting on other people's posts. This builds their awareness of you and keeps you front of mind.

… AND GET TO KNOW YOUR CONNECTIONS

Remember, it's not all about you. Just like any relationship, there is give and take. When someone accepts your invitation to connect or asks to connect with you, don't just accept it and move on. Be curious. Ask them questions. My own research shows that about 50% of people who connect with you on LinkedIn do so because they need help – if not now, at some stage in the future. So, talk to them. Find out what their goals are and see if you can help. Offer them advice and follow up with them.

Another great tip is to keep an eye on the people who frequently like and comment on your posts. Reach out to them, thank them for their comments and let them know you're available to chat any time they need help. It will strengthen the connection you have with them and could result in more business and leads.

CONNECT THROUGH GROUPS

LinkedIn allows you to be a member of up to 50 groups. Think of all the like-minded people and potential leads you can connect with! You can also join private and public groups on Facebook. Comment on posts and engage in the conversation. Share your thoughts and expertise. This will help grow your network and raise your profile.

LEVERAGE YOUR PROFILE FOR EVENTS

LinkedIn allows you to get a lot of the hard work out of the way before you attend an event. In the lead-up to the day, check whether the organisers are using a hashtag on Twitter. Keep an eye on who is posting in the Twitter feed, then try to find them on LinkedIn and send them a request to connect. If they accept, you'll have some people lined up to talk to on the day.

For example, your connection request could say: "Hi! I noticed you're attending the leadership conference in a couple of weeks. I'd love to catch up with you. I just wanted to introduce myself here so I could keep an eye out for you on the day. I hope that's OK with you."

Don't forget to touch base with the people you meet at events within 24 hours. Look for them on your social networks and link up to keep the conversation, and awareness, going.

ONLINE, TV AND PRINT MEDIA ADVERTISING

I'm often asked whether it's worth investing in social media ads and other forms of advertising to reach out to people. Digital technology is evolving fast and there are some great opportunities for online marketing and building awareness. The challenge with this type of advertising is it's easy to lose a lot of money if you don't know what you're doing.

Kirsty Saint is one of my good friends and the master writer for our LinkedIn profiles. Kirsty is a Facebook Ads guru and has worked with many of our Influencer clients, so she sees the advertising pitfalls and opportunities people often miss.

Kirsty runs Facebook marketing campaigns for a broad range of small businesses, yet is one of the few experts who also understands the Influencer industry. So, I decided to ask Kirsty about the potential of Facebook advertising for Influencers.

INDUSTRY INFLUENCER SPOTLIGHT
KIRSTY SAINT: FACEBOOK ADVERTISING

Kirsty Saint is a Facebook Certified Professional, a credential for those recognised as having advanced-level proficiency in Facebook's family of products and services. She is also a digital content strategist who works closely with me and my team on LinkedIn, writing many of our clients' profiles for maximum impact and lead generation.

1. Why use Facebook Ads for business growth and lead generation?

With 2 billion users, Facebook is the largest social media network on the planet. As an advertising platform, it crosses the divide from cookie-based marketing to cross-device, people-based marketing. This gives Facebook a competitive advantage, due to the granularity of its targeting capabilities.

Facebook harnesses artificial intelligence so it can deliver the content its users want to see. Unlike cookies (used for display ads and search-based platforms such as Google AdWords), Facebook uses what's known as "Pixel".

Facebook uses the data from your ad account's Pixel to continually update its algorithm on the types of people who take certain actions on your site or engage with your page or posts, regardless of the device. It knows their demographics and, most importantly, their interests. It also knows which other people share the same interests and are likely to take the desired action from your ads.

Facebook can help you get in front of specific and often motivated segments of your audience with powerful ad targeting options you've probably never even heard of.

Users can be targeted using a dizzying array of options: pages followed, connections to your page, interests, job titles, employer, industry, income, education, purchase behaviour, how often they travel internationally, whether they're early technology adopters, and even what type of car they drive. Facebook also allows categories of people to be excluded from your audience targeting.

Importantly, once you find an audience on Facebook that converts (this can even be your own customer list), you can clone them into a "lookalike audience". Facebook will then reach new people outside your network who are similar to that audience and likely to be interested in your business.

2. What is the benefit of Facebook Ads for Influencers?

For Influencers, coaches, mentors, speakers and authors, Facebook Ads can be an incredibly valuable tool to build your network and move new clients through your sales funnel.

Many Influencers already invest time and energy into a Facebook business page, but unfortunately the days of organic reach on Facebook are long gone. Every time you post on Facebook, that post reaches less than 10% of your followers!

Although other platforms such as LinkedIn are valuable for making connections and nurturing your network, there simply isn't the same ability to target and move people through your sales funnel at scale.

Facebook also has a large variety of ad types and objectives, allowing you to choose the desired outcome. This may depend on whether you want to establish your personal brand with a new audience, or convert those who already have an established relationship with you into a program or event.

3. Are Facebook Ads expensive?

Facebook is one of – if not the most – powerful advertising platforms available today. And consequently, that doesn't come cheaply. You need to invest money to receive a return.

You may have heard about one-cent link clicks, but what you may not realise is that the most successful advertisers run long-term, relationship-building campaigns before they are able to find success with such a low-cost option. They spend time and money to create a campaign, refine their audience, split test creatives and optimise for results.

How much to invest in Facebook Ads depends on your objective. If it's only to add 100 more potential clients to your email database, it will cost a lot less than a conversion campaign to sign people up to a $5,000 program or event.

Ask yourself how much one new client is worth to your business over the lifetime you'll work with them. Would it be $5,000? $50,000?

To determine your initial ad-spend budget for the first month, I usually recommend allocating 10% of the profit you would make from one new client to your business, or the value of a certain number of people added to your email list. This budget will allow for split testing and optimisation to gain a true indication of what each conversion costs your business. A proficient Facebook Ads manager will ensure continued optimisation, lowest ad spend and greatest ROI.

Remember, a 10x or even 5x return on investment from any source is great. Facebook is no different. It's not about how much or how little you spend on ads; it's about the value you receive in return.

However, compared to advertising on other platforms, such as LinkedIn or Google AdWords, Facebook is usually considerably cheaper – sometimes up to seven times cheaper!

4. I notice that Facebook says I can boost a post on my page for $25. Can't I just do that?

Every Facebook page owner sees the blue buttons that appear near their posts or on their page, with the tempting offer to spend just $10 or $25 to reach more people. The one and only objective of a boosted post is to reach as many people who will engage with likes, comments and shares as possible. It doesn't optimise for link clicks, video views, sign ups or conversions.

It allows for some interest targeting, but not exclusions. It doesn't allow you to optimise with granular targeting to reach those who will take the action you would like on your post, eg. provide their email address in return for a free download. When page owners find their $25 does not achieve these actions, they often conclude that Facebook advertising doesn't work.

To harness the true capabilities of Facebook Ads, you need to move your advertising dollars from your page to Facebook's Business Manager platform. This is where you can create, analyse, refine and optimise to make the magic of Facebook Ads happen.

Within Business Manager, advertisers can:

- Create and split test different ad formats and components, such as imagery, content, headline and targeting.
- Create interest-based targeted audiences, custom audiences of existing followers or clients, and lookalike audiences.
- Assess and optimise ad and campaign performance via metrics such as click-through rates (CTR), cost per click (CPC), relevance and cost per action.

5. What are the pitfalls of Facebook Ads for Influencers?

Facebook Ads requires more knowledge than simply how to create a well-written ad with an engaging image. To truly harness its power, you must understand how to analyse the audience and performance metrics to continually optimise your campaigns. Or else you could work with a Facebook Ads specialist who does.

Be aware that it takes time for a campaign to get results and up to seven days to optimise. Best practice involves split testing, refining the audience and re-targeting. You may need to allow up to four weeks to see your desired results.

Not spending enough is a potential pitfall. Advertisers who limit their Facebook Ads spend to a couple of hundred dollars per campaign will see minimal results.

Advertising on Facebook doesn't mean you can neglect relationships. Making calls and meeting people are still a large part of the sales cycle for Influencers who advertise on Facebook.

In today's competitive marketplace, it is rare for a cold audience to purchase a high-value program or service directly from any ad. If you sell a product or service worth $2,000 or above, your funnel will usually need to include one-on-one contact with prospects.

6. What should Influencers have before they start Facebook Ads campaigns?

Before setting up your Facebook campaigns, have ad collateral ready, such as a range of images to split test and, ideally, videos, which can be captioned within Facebook's ad platform. Ensure what you have is

> high quality, engaging and creative. For Influencers, the most successful Facebook campaigns are those that are supported by a funnel, which may be as simple as: Ad > Lead Magnet > Retarget with Offer > Upsell or Book a Call. The funnel can also be more complicated with webinars or a longer awareness and engagement-building timeframe.
>
> You will need to have landing pages optimised for your calls to action and the Facebook Pixel installed on these web pages, as well as any third-party platforms in use, such as Eventbrite.
>
> You need to commit to an adequate advertising budget for your ad spend, determined by the value each lead or conversion is worth to your business.
>
> Finally, ensure you have a good understanding of how Facebook Ads works before setting up your first campaign, or engage a Facebook Ads specialist who does.

REFERRALS

Referrals are gold, yet they remain an untapped resource for so many professionals. Even when the service you deliver is outstanding, you can't expect referrals to simply roll in (although it's nice when they do!).

As an Influencer, you need to take the lead and actively pursue referrals by reaching out to your networks.

IF YOU DON'T ASK, YOU DON'T GET

> *"Ask for what you want and be prepared to get it."*
> *- Maya Angelou*

People are often so busy that they're unable to think outside their own hectic worlds. Your clients, acquaintances and contacts may know of many people who need your help, but the idea of connecting them with you simply hasn't entered their minds. It's up to you to approach your contacts for leads.

Don't feel sheepish about asking people for referrals. You may worry that you'll come across as pushy and salesy. But relax. If you have a positive, respectful relationship with your contacts, they will be glad to help.

Asking for referrals also gives them a little ego boost. It shows that you regard them highly enough to ask for their help and advice, and they will find pleasure in being "in the know". People love to feel important!

Keep the ball rolling with your satisfied customers. If you receive a complimentary email from a client, respond with: "Thank you. I'm so pleased you're happy with my work. Do you know anyone else who could benefit from my services?"

Set yourself a goal for the number of referrals you'd like to generate each week. Take targeted steps to achieve them by contacting the people in your networks.

MOMENTS OF TRUTH

My partner Mark and I recently saw the movie *Hidden Figures*. It tells the story of Katherine Johnson and two of her colleagues – three brilliant female African-American mathematicians working for NASA in the 1960s. (Warning: Spoiler alert ahead!)

Johnson was incredibly bright and gifted, and was promoted to a critical role where she helped NASA with its US space program – including sending astronaut John Glenn into space. The challenge was to get Glenn, whose life was at risk, and his spacecraft safely back to Earth. Without Johnson's mathematical expertise, Glenn may never have made it back in time. And if that happened, the future of NASA and its space program would have been jeopardised.

Despite Johnson's indomitable intelligence, what was really hindering NASA's operation was the inherent racism and sexism endemic to US society in the mid-20th century. This was a time when race segregation still existed, which was highlighted in the movie by the fact that the African American women's bathroom was located in another building away from the central workplace. Johnson had to walk about a kilometre from her office building to use it because she was not allowed to use the white women's bathroom. NASA's culture of unconscious bias was not only impeding the nation's progress as it tried to beat the Russians into space – it was putting lives at risk.

It wasn't until Johnson's boss Al Harrison (played by Kevin Costner) said, "Where is she? She's always missing," that things started to shift. When he realised the reason why Johnson was so often absent – the long walk she had to endure simply to use the bathroom – he ripped down the "white women's bathroom only" sign. "Katherine will be using this bathroom," he declared. That moment in the movie was a moment of truth.

CHAPTER 5.3

In his book, *The Hero's Journey*, Joseph Campbell talks about how the most captivating movies and stories involve a hero's journey. There is a moment in the hero's journey, usually half-way through the story, that's known as "a moment of truth". It's the moment where something changes. It's a turning point, a catalyst for everything else to come. This was certainly the case in *Hidden Figures*. Harrison ripping the sign off the white women's bathroom was the moment of truth that led to the success of NASA's space program. Who would have thought that a toilet sign was the thing that was holding up the ultimate success of the US space program?

The key point to remember is that the moment of truth happens halfway through a movie, not at the end. It's the catalyst that makes everything work. The same thing happens in business. Let's explore this idea.

In 2003, Fred Reichheld, from Bain & Company and Satmetrix Systems, introduced the concept of the Net Promoter Score (NPS) in the *Harvard Business Review*.[2] Today, it is one of the most widely used metrics to gauge customer loyalty. The score is correlated with business growth. A score can be as high as +100 or as low as -100. A score higher than zero is considered good and a score of more than 50 is considered excellent. The score is based on one question: *"How likely is it that you would recommend our company/product/service to a friend or colleague?"*

I was recently speaking with a sales manager about the NPS, who said, "Our team has the highest scores of our firm's customer service ratings. When we ask our customers if they would refer someone else to us, the answer is 'yes' every time. We score 10 out of 10. But the key issue is, we don't actually ask for that referral. When that data comes through, it comes through fairly late in the process. For us to then go back and ask our customers for that referral, it feels a bit awkward and uncomfortable. So, we don't do it."

However, we know that those referrals are so important. In fact, it was the author of the book *The Referral Engine*, John Jantsch, who said: "In the business of referrals, trust is the most important reason a recommendation is made, and conversely, lack of trust is the single reason referrals don't happen."

So, the real issue with translating NPS into lead generation is understanding our *moments of truth*. The moments when our customers feel our impact the most and are emotionally driven. "Wow factor" moments, when a client has a breakthrough, when they receive an insight or successful outcome they weren't expecting because of working with you – that's their moment of truth. That's when they're on a high, their reciprocity bank is unbalanced and they

---

2 "The One Number You Need to Grow," *Harvard Business Review*, December 2003, https://hbr.org/2003/12/the-one-number-you-need-to-grow

are most likely to refer you to others. You need to be attuned to and act upon these moments of truth as they happen throughout your "story" with your customer, not at the end when you're busy reporting. If you wait until the end to ask for referrals, it's too late.

There are moments of truth in your business and in your practice when the timing is right to ask for an outbound referral. "Do you know someone else who has this same issue who I could help?" Now, the problem is we usually ask this question when we need it, such as a testimonial when we're creating a testimonials page on our website. Or we may ask it in a moment of panic after a trigger event, such as a sales meeting, when we realise, "Oh no, what are we going to do to fill our pipeline?"

So, ask yourself: What are the moments of truth in your practice? What mechanisms do you have in place to capture referrals, testimonials and LinkedIn recommendations? It's essential that you harness the power of your moments of truth so you can increase the amount of trust in your business, capture more leads and have a greater impact on the potential clients who need your help.

Oh, and yes – go see the movie!

For experts, coaching sessions and workshops are fantastic ways of getting referrals. If you're delivering a mentoring or coaching session, ask the attendees if they know of anyone else who may need your help. Feedback forms are an easy way to do this. Simply include a field on the form asking, "Is there anyone you can recommend who might benefit from this session?"

SPEAK

> *"Every time you have to speak, you are auditioning for leadership."*
> *– James Humes*

Public speaking is a golden ticket to creating awareness and generating leads. It's where you can truly let your personality and expertise shine. It's also great for gaining an insight into your audience's problems, which is crucial for refining your services. Yet surveys about people's fears commonly show that public speaking is at the top of the list!

American comedian Jerry Seinfeld sees the funny side to this perplexing situation: "People's number-one fear is public speaking. Number two is death. Death is number two. Does that sound right? This means to the average person, if you go to a funeral, you're better off in the casket than doing the eulogy." So true, isn't it?

CHAPTER 5.3

Fear doesn't discriminate. You may be someone who has achieved phenomenal success in your professional career, yet quake at the thought of speaking in front of an audience. I know, I've been there. I was terrified the first time I spoke in front of a group of people. It was 2002 and I had to teach an audience of 20 people one of the most basic things you can think of – how to tie a shoelace! Now, tying a shoelace is something I've been doing automatically since childhood, but I was scared to death about explaining it to a group strangers!

Here are five ways to build your confidence as a public speaker and ensure your presentations are a hit:

1. **Know your key message.** What message do you want your audience to walk away with? Keep the goal of your presentation at the front of your mind when writing and delivering your speech. It will keep your message focused so you don't go off track.

2. **Tell stories.** Personal stories help create a bond between you and your audience. Look for emotional anchors that will resonate with others to nurture their faith in you. For example, a client in one of my workshops needed to explain to his team that they should be mindful of their spending and keep a close watch of their resources. He related his own story of when he was a university student, working three jobs to make ends meet. Every dollar he made counted. It was an effective story his team members could relate to.

3. **Speak clearly.** Don't talk too fast or too quietly. The audience will find it hard to follow and quickly lose interest. Clear enunciation is key. If you're not easily understood, your message will fail to make an impact and you will quickly lose confidence in your own abilities.

4. **Invest in good-quality graphics.** Photos, infographics and illustrations command attention and help your messages stick. They guide people through what you're saying and give them something to focus on so they don't "zone out". Choose one image per slide, ensuring that it's clearly visible. Stick to high-resolution images (300dpi). A low-resolution image (72dpi) can appear blurry when blown up on a large screen, and it's embarrassing when you have to say to your audience, "I'm not sure if you can see this in the graph, but …"

5. **Emphasise points one at a time.** Overcrowding your slides with information will confuse your audience. You're also more likely to go off track if you try to juggle too many points at once. Focus on one point per slide.

And, of course, you must practice, practice, practice!

HOW TO POSITION YOURSELF AS A SPEAKER

To get speaking engagements, you need to position yourself as a speaker. Create touchpoints that will help event managers and facilitators see you as a leader in your field.

To build awareness of your speaking expertise, you must:

- **Create a SAM website.** Matt Church, founder of Thought Leaders Global, says a SAM (speaker, author, mentor) website is essential to positioning yourself as an expert in your industry. Simply adding a speaker page to an existing business website won't have the same kind of impact. You need a separate website to make a lasting impression, and it needs to be under your name.com. List companies you've worked for (include their logos for validity) and events you've spoken at. Include testimonials, as well as photos and videos of you speaking. If you haven't spoken at many – or any – events yet, film yourself. You need to provide evidence that you can speak effectively. And make sure you constantly update and refine your website. You're less likely to get speaking gigs if the information on your website is outdated.

- **Write a book.** Books build trust. They are a powerful way of emphasising your extensive knowledge and help people get to know you and your message. If you're in the middle of writing your book or about to start, you don't need to wait until you have finished to organise the cover design. Get a cover created early and use it everywhere you can – on your home page, website banners, social media and promotional material. You want to generate interest in your book as early as possible.

- **Say yes.** If someone asks you to speak, start speaking! It doesn't matter how small the event is, you need to get as many speaking engagements under your belt as possible. And be prepared to do a lot of unpaid speaking to get the ball rolling. Neil McCallum, one of my early speaking coaches, once said to me, "Come back and talk to me when you've done 250 gigs. Then you're really ready to start talking about some more paid speaking." So, that's what I did! I aimed for volume, did my 250 speaking events, and my career as a keynote skyrocketed.

- **Create a flyer.** Create a keynote speaker flyer that people can download from your website. This shows that you're serious and speaking is not a side gig for you. Include your speaking topics, a brief bio and list any inclusions with your presentations – for example, information sheets, workbooks and access to your webinars and podcasts.

- **Share images of you speaking.** Whenever you speak at an event, organise someone to take photos of you on stage and share them on your social media accounts to build awareness. Include images of you speaking in your profile banners. Get a designer to create a custom LinkedIn background image for your profile that includes a high-quality image of you speaking.

- **Create calls to action.** Make it as easy as possible for others to engage you as a speaker. Use your email signature to make it clear that you're available to speak. Include a hyperlinked tagline. For example, "To get John to speak at your next event, click here." Put this tagline in your e-newsletters and letterheads. Seize every opportunity you can to build awareness.

- **Ask for referrals.** Put a call out on social media. I always get enquiries whenever I create a post asking people if they'd like me to speak at their next event. If you've delivered a keynote, remember to ask the event manager, "Do you know of anyone else who runs events I might be able to help by delivering a session for them?"

RECORD EVERYTHING

Organise a recording every time you speak. This builds your collateral so event managers will have the confidence that you know what you're doing. Hire a professional videographer and photographer to record your speaking engagements. Their footage and images will be priceless to you as you develop your positioning.

SHARE YOUR KEYNOTES

Share whole keynotes or snippets of your speaking engagements to build awareness of what you do. Every time you speak, upload something to social media. Obsess over it. Australian keynote speaker Bernard Salt is a great example of this. Every time he speaks, he gets someone to take a photo of him on stage and he posts it on Facebook. In his post, he's specific about how many delegates he spoke to, what the topic was and where the event was held.

It's also important that you let people know you regularly travel for your speaking engagements. Post a "selfie" as you're about to hop on a plane to speak at an interstate event. It shows that location is no barrier for you as a speaker.

RUN A WEBINAR

A few years ago, there was a change of legislation in self-managed superannuation funds, which created compliance implications for financial advisers in Australia. At the time, my team was creating LinkedIn profiles for a financial organisation's staff. We noticed that there was little information about the changes coming through on LinkedIn, so we recommended to the client that they run a webinar. So they did, and as a result achieved more than 500 new leads!

Webinars are one of the best ways to access new markets and new revenue streams. They are lead-generating machines, allowing you to create awareness in new markets and educate your existing client base. They're perfect for weeks when you don't have speaking engagements, so that you're still progressing your positioning as a speaker without standing on a stage. Webinars are also a wonderful way to build your confidence if you're still feeling a bit uncomfortable about speaking in front of a live audience.

Essentially, a webinar is a seminar, presentation or information session that is conducted over the internet. It's transmitted using video-conferencing software that allows you to share audio, video, documents and applications with your online audience. It's different to a podcast or webcast in that it allows interaction between you and the attendees.

For your first webinar, you probably won't get a huge number of people registering. Often, only 30%-50% of people who do register attend the session. Don't be disheartened! It's important that you go ahead with your webinar as planned. Record it to build your collateral. Get it transcribed and use it to create blog posts, articles and even your own book.

There are three elements to creating a successful webinar:

1. MARKETING

- **What is the purpose of your webinar?** You want your webinar to boost awareness of what you do, but there may be other things you want to achieve as well: for example, more coaching clients, workshop registrations or book sales. Understanding your goal will help you decide how to market your webinar and who to market it to.

    Remember, people generally need to consume 10 pieces of content (eg. blog posts, reviews, social media posts) before they decide to work with you. Your webinar will help them trust you, but now is not the time to go for the hard sell.

Your goal doesn't have to be centred on sales. If most of the people who register for your webinar are new leads, they probably will not buy from you yet anyway. If you do want to achieve a certain amount of sales for a product or service, promote your webinar to people who are already in your sales funnel. You'll be more likely to clinch sales with people who have previously had a positive experience working with you.

- **Where does your target audience hang out?** Are they on LinkedIn, Facebook or Twitter? What groups are they a part of? This information is critical to knowing where to promote your webinar. Reach out to your networks and invite them to register.

- **Landing page.** Create a landing page on your website that entices people to sign up to your webinar. Your landing page should address the following:

    - Your audience's problems and fears.
    - Topics you'll cover.
    - An image of their world – something that is relevant and familiar.
    - Who you are and why people should listen to you. Remember to include your picture. You could also create a video explaining who you are and how you can help.
    - What others have said about working with you.
    - Who you have worked with – eg. brands, industries, organisations and clients.
    - Provide ample opportunity for people to register throughout the copy. Link to your registration page wherever possible and include a highly visible call-to-action button.

    Link to your landing page in your social media pages, e-newsletters and email signature. For a basic sample landing page, take a look at https://janeandersonspeaks.com/linkedin-for-research-translation/

- **Registration page.** Set up your webinar registration page in the platform you're using – eg. GoToWebinar, WebinarNinja, WebinarJam. Include required fields, such as email address, full name and mobile number, so you can add their information to your client database.

2. **DELIVERY**

- **Choose your webinar software or platform.** There are numerous options available, some of which are free and some are paid. To name a few: GoToWebinar, WebinarJam, Google+ Hangout, Skype, Cisco WebEx, ReadyTalk, Adobe Connect, AnyMeeting, ClickWebinar.

- **Decide on the structure and write your content.** Australian marketing guru Taki Moore offers fantastic advice on how to structure your webinar effectively. You want your webinar to deliver great-value information to your audience, but you don't want them to walk away and not act on it. To make sure your webinar has maximum effect, Moore says you need to:

  - **Set the scene.** Show your audience that if they do something wrong, something bad will happen. Be specific with the details and present the negative outcomes. Then, show what wonderful things will happen when they do the right thing. Again, be specific with the details of these positive outcomes.

  - **Prove your case.** If you don't back your claims with evidence, people won't believe you. Use testimonials, statistics and case studies to substantiate what you're saying. You need to prove that what you're saying works in the real world.

  - **Make your content personal.** Use personal language so your audience makes the connection between your theory and themselves. Ask them a direct question that requires an answer. Make it crystal clear that they have a choice to do nothing and make the same mistakes over and over, or commit to your program to achieve life-changing results.

- **Interact with your audience using polls and surveys.**
  This is a great way to take your webinar to the next level. It keeps people engaged and online, and can give you a valuable insight into your audience's needs and problems. You can create multiple-question and "rate-on-a-scale" polls and surveys that you can send out while you're talking. You can choose to show your audience the
  results immediately or at the end of the webinar to keep them guessing.

3. **POST DELIVERY**

- **Follow up with your audience so you don't lose momentum.** Allocate time in your calendar for follow-up calls and emails – ideally, within 24 hours of the webinar. You want to make contact as soon as you can so your audience doesn't forget you and move on to the next thing. Ask them if there were points raised that resonated with them, and if they have any challenges you can help them with. If you conducted a poll or survey during the webinar, analyse the results and use them as a launching pad to connect with attendees.

For more information on conducting webinars, check out *Webinar Smarts* by Perth-based business consultant and speaker Gihan Perera. It covers nearly everything you need to know about producing high-quality webinars that raise people's awareness of what you do. Find out more about the e-book here: https://www.amazon.com.au/Webinar-Smarts-Gihan-Perera-ebook/dp/B007Y1I1UE

INDUSTRY INFLUENCER SPOTLIGHT
VICKY SAUNDERS: SPORTS SPONSORSHIP EXPERT

1. You created a challenge for yourself to speak to 10,000 people for free in a quarter. Can you tell us about why you did that? Was it to achieve sales, visibility, etc.?

I had three reasons for wanting to speak to 10,000 people:

1. To increase my network and database.
2. To increase and improve my profile.
3. To improve my public-speaking skills and test out new ideas.

And, of course, all three of those things should at some point lead to sales!

I already knew from previous media coverage that media alone doesn't often convert directly to sales, but what you do with that media can be incredibly valuable. So, my intention from the start was to not only speak to 10K people, but to share those speaking activities with my existing social media network to further engage them and increase my credibility in their eyes.

2. How did you do it?

I wrote a list of all the different ways I could get in front of people, such as podcasts, live events (ones that I organised as well as others' events, such as expos), radio, television, etc. Luckily, I had a book launch in Singapore organised by my clients Deloitte and Singapore Sport, and they arranged for more than 12 national media companies to attend.

I also created my own podcasts and videos and kept track of how many views they had. I quickly achieved my target of 10K, and I stopped counting when I reached more than 3 million. I realised that the sky is the limit and I could get obsessed with hitting new targets, but it wouldn't necessarily improve my business.

By speaking at events, I collected lots of business cards and added them to my database. I shared everything via social media and my engagement, particularly on LinkedIn, has skyrocketed. People I meet for the first time now tell me they saw me on TV or they saw my post about my work with the US Olympic Committee. So, without me telling them anything, they already know good things about me. It really helps establish a good reputation and a sense of rapport without even having met before.

3. Did you achieve growth in your sales?

Not directly, but yes. My sales tripled in the final quarter of 2016 and now going into 2017, my first half of the year is going to be twice as profitable as all of 2015.

No new clients have said, "Hi, I saw you on TV and now want to spend money with you," but it gave me much more engagement with my existing database, and the conversations with clients since then have been so much easier as they either saw all the speaking events and activities I was doing, have heard my podcast (or a colleague has recommended it to them), and instantly I have credibility and don't need to prove or explain myself. We can go straight into the discussion about "what" work they want me to do rather than "if" they want me to work with them.

Some events I spoke at have resulted in work with people from the audience, but more often it is a networking opportunity, which is valuable to me in so many ways.

4. What did you learn?

That having a goal and a strategy are incredibly powerful: one drives you and one directs you. I loved the challenge of reaching 10,000 people and thought it would be more difficult than it was, but when I offered to speak, most people said yes! The key was repurposing the content and sharing the experiences and activities across social media – LinkedIn, Facebook, Twitter – and sending emails to my database, letting them know what I was up to.

CHAPTER 5.3

QUESTIONS FOR YOU TO CONSIDER:

1. If you could reach out to anyone as an ideal client, who would they be? Can you find them on LinkedIn? What can you say to reach out and connect with them?

   _____
   _____
   _____

2. Which Facebook and LinkedIn groups can you engage in conversation with to raise your profile?

   _____
   _____
   _____

3. How many referrals would you like to generate each week? Who are 10 people you could ask for referrals?

   _____
   _____
   _____

4. What handouts do you give out when you speak at conferences and events to gain referrals?

   _____
   _____
   _____

5. Have you set up your website with your name as the domain name? Does it include your speaker kit and show reel?

   _____
   _____

6. Have a look through your social media feed for the past three weeks. How many times have you featured yourself as a speaker, sharing images of yourself speaking on stage?

   _____
   _____

7. Have you run a webinar before? If not, have you been an audience member of a webinar? What did you notice, good and bad? If you ran one yourself, what would it be about? Who might you invite? What problems do they need help with?

_____
_____
_____
_____
_____

8. What other proactive reaching-out marketing strategies have you undertaken? Which ones were the most successful?

_____
_____
_____

9. Where does your ideal client hang out the most? Could you get in front of a group of them in a keynote or webinar?

_____
_____
_____

10. How many people on your database are your ideal clients?

_____
_____
_____

11. How many more do you need to get to 3200?

_____
_____

12. If you were to set yourself a goal of speaking to 10,000 people within the next 90 days, what ideas come to mind for you to achieve that goal?

_____
_____
_____

13. When you speak, what percentage of the room do you acquire contact details from?

_____
_____
_____

14. How many speaking events are booked in your calendar for the year ahead? (Hint: Ideally, it should be one per month to one per week.)

_____
_____
_____

15. How often do you ask your clients for referrals?

_____
_____
_____

16. How do you go about asking them?

_____
_____
_____
_____

17. What holds you back from asking?

_____
_____
_____
_____

18. When do you ask? At the end of the transaction or while you're working together?

_____
_____
_____
_____

19. Write down the five most recent clients who have achieved success from working with you. Write down a time you will contact them this week to ask for a testimonial or recommendation.

_____
_____
_____
_____
_____

20. How will you use the information you have read in this chapter?

_____
_____
_____
_____
_____

CHAPTER 5.3

CHAPTER 5.4

Educate

"Education is the most powerful weapon which you can use to change the world."
– Nelson Mandela

In this digital age, consumers are more knowledgeable than ever. With a few keystrokes, they have access to a plethora of information to help them decide what to buy and who to work with. It's an incredibly empowering era. The problem is, so much of the information out there is unhelpful, misguided and irrelevant.

There is a world of difference between marketing to your audience and educating them. Simply listing the features of your services is not enough. It's too promotional and offers no insight. People tune out because they think, "What's that got to do with me? Why should I care?"

As an Influencer, you need to explain to your clients what their problems are. Clearly demonstrate how you can solve them. What are the benefits of your services? What issues do they resolve? What outcomes can you achieve and what process is involved?

You must *prove* that what you offer is indispensable. Educating your audience is the best way to do this. As *Forbes* says, "The more informed and empowered customers are, the more satisfied and confident they are with their choices. And that kind of confidence almost always leads to loyalty."[1]

information they need to decide whether to buy from you or work with you. Often, they don't even realise they have a need or an issue. It's your job to make them aware and educate them. And your ability to teach them nurtures their trust in you.

For example, at Athlete's Foot, you can't simply walk into a store and choose a new pair of shoes. You're encouraged to get a foot and gait analysis using their video, pressure and fitting screen technology. A camera films you walking on a platform while sensors examine your foot pressure. You get to view the

---

[1] "Don't Market to Your Customers; Educate Them Instead." *Forbes*, April 10, 2015, http://www.forbes.com/sites/williamcraig/2015/04/10/dont-market-to-your-customers-educate-them-instead/#505442504f61

way you walk and are shown where you place the most pressure on your feet. The results are analysed and explained to you so you know what kind of foot shape you have, whether you under-pronate or over-pronate, and whether or not you would benefit from orthotics. You're then presented with multiple pairs of shoes that fit your foot support requirements.

Basically, the staff arms you with knowledge so you can make an informed decision about what shoes to buy.

This approach works wonders because it shows that the store treats each customer as an individual. The customer is made aware of and educated about any underlying issues, and is presented with multiple solutions. All of this means they are more likely to trust the store and come back next time they need shoes.

Be generous with the information you share. Don't give it with the expectation you will get something in return. Educating comes back to having an honest desire to help people. True leaders and Influencers genuinely want to change the lives of their audiences for the better. Delivering valuable, relevant and educational content is the key.

Let's explore the three activities related to the Educate quadrant:

- Podcast
- Social Media Posts
- Blog

PODCAST

Podcasts have been around since the early 1930s in the form of radio shows. The term "podcast" was first used by Ben Hammersley in *The Guardian* in February 2004, along with other names for the new media platform. Since then, podcasts have been created in almost any genre and topic you can think of!

Podcasting is an intimate way for you to connect with your audience. It brings you into their lives at a very personal level, as you can't skim content or headlines as you would with other digital and printed media. A podcast is an easy, convenient way for people to consume your content. Unlike text and video, a podcast doesn't require the undivided attention of your audience. People can listen to podcasts anywhere – while they're on their daily commute, exercising or in the park on their lunch break, which means you can reach more people and have more impact with your message.

A podcast keeps things interesting. You can add music and voice overs. You can have regular guests and interview experts in your field, which help with your networking and adds authenticity to your brand. And you can become more intimate with your audience while educating them in an informal yet memorable way.

What's more, relatively few businesses do it. This means you'll stand head and shoulders above your competitors if you have a podcast.

To access a podcast, listeners will generally go to the iTunes or Google Play podcast store and search for your name or via a category. Here are some interesting statistics that reveal why podcasting is powerful for taking you from an expert to an Influencer:

- 21% of Americans ages 12 and up have listened to a podcast in the past month. This is up from 17% in 2015. Monthly podcast listenership has increased by more than 75% since 2013.

- The podcast audience in the US is 57 million, and 56% of those are men and 44% are women.

- 51% of listeners have a four-year degree or higher, with 41% earning more than $75,000 per year and 21% earning more than $100,000 per year.

- Podcasts are driven by mobility. When podcasting first started, most were listened to on a computer. Today, more than 64% of podcasts are listened to on a mobile device. People are listening to podcasts on a commute, at the gym, while exercising outdoors and in the car.

- Weekly podcast listeners consume five shows per week on average. This number directly correlates with most of the daily activities people engage in – a daily gym session or commute to work, for example. More than 52% of listeners listen in the car, 46% listen while traveling on planes, 40% listen while walking, running and biking, 37% listen while they are on public transport and 32% listen while they work out.

- According to Jay Baer, one of the most popular marketing and social media Influencers, the sweet spot for podcasting is five times per week. My experience speaking with Australian audiences is that too many podcasts can feel a little noisy. So even if you start with just one podcast episode per week, you'll be ahead of the game!

CHAPTER 5.4

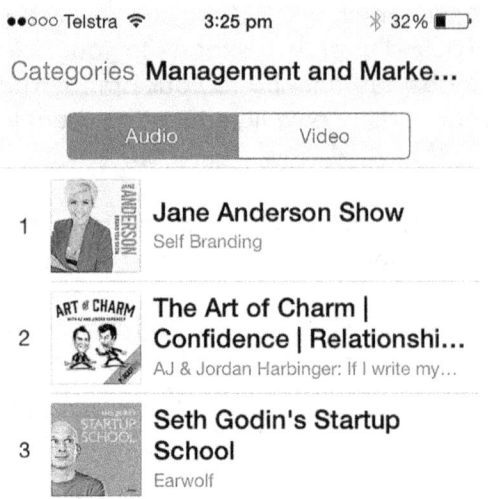

Management and Marketing Category #1 spot!

- Podcasters are also highly social, with 75% being on Facebook, 41% being on Instagram, 36% on Twitter and 33% on LinkedIn.

WHAT DO YOU NEED TO DO TO START A PODCAST?

The best place to start is by getting clear about your message and who your ideal listener is. You need to identify their different traits, such as:

- Male and/or female, and age group
- Married, single or in a relationship
- Salary
- Location
- Type of work they do
- Level within an organisation
- Industry
- Hobbies, passions and interests

Once you know this information, you can start to align your program with your other content, such as videos and blogs.

HOW TO CREATE A PODCAST

Ensure you have the right equipment. Having poor sound quality will reduce your downloads and the number of people listening to you, so invest in the right equipment. Essentially, you'll need a high-quality microphone and software to create your audio file. Technology changes fast, so I won't list them here. I recommend checking my website and blog for the most recent post on how to run your podcast with the latest equipment: https://janeandersonspeaks.com/blog/

Here is a high-level overview that can give you a sense of how to get started:

1. **Create your episode.** Your podcast episode can be as long as you like. Most recommendations are anywhere from 20 minutes to one hour, which is the amount of time for a typical commute, walk or gym session. Once you have created your podcast recording, you need to ensure it has an introduction and perhaps some music. This is, essentially, your audio branding, reminding people what the purpose of your podcast is and who you serve. You don't have to do this yourself, of course. You can pay someone from freelancing sites such as Fiverr.com and Upwork.com to do it for you if you're unsure. If you prefer to do this yourself, you can use tools such as Camtasia, which is helpful if you're doing videos as well.

2. **You now have an audio file.** Perfect! You've got an audio file, now you need to publish that to your podcast so people can access it, download it and listen to it. How that all works is centered around something called the RSS feed. An RSS feed is basically a text file that contains all the details of the podcast. If you look at one, you'll notice it looks like a lot of computer code. This is a data delivery language called XML, which contains everything about your podcast – title, description, who the author is, the links to the artwork, and links to the actual audio files themselves. It provides a kind of URL to where the podcast episodes live on the internet. When you talk about submitting your podcast to iTunes, for example, all you're really doing is providing iTunes with the link to that RSS feed. This means that whenever any changes are made to it or a new episode is uploaded, iTunes keeps checking back to that RSS feed and updates the store accordingly. Then, when people subscribe to the podcast, they're subscribing to that feed as well. For example, if you've got your podcast in the iTunes store, and I log in to the iTunes store with my account and subscribe to a podcast, what my account does is continually check back to your RSS feed for any updates and new episodes. When a new episode is uploaded, it automatically appears in my account. So, when you're creating a podcast, you need to create that feed somehow, and the easiest way to do that is by using a podcast hosting system.

3. **Upload your file into your podcast hosting platform.** There are many podcast hosting services available, such as Libsyn, SoundCloud, Whooshkaa and Blubrry, to name a few. It's worth doing a shop around to compare the different services. While they will all create an RSS feed for you, some offer valuable tools, such as analytics that measure who's listening to your podcast, how long they're listening for and how many

downloads you're getting. Some services offer a review tracker that tracks what people are saying about your podcast through iTunes.

4. **Upload into iTunes and you're ready to go!** Once you have created an iTunes account, you can upload your recording into iTunes from your hosting platform. Leverage your podcast as much as you can across all your social media platforms and newsletter list. You're well and truly on your way to creating even higher levels of trust in your practice! Ensure you measure your data, monitoring the number of downloads and locations of your listeners. Always have a call to action in your podcast to encourage listeners to subscribe or access resources from your website.

LINKS:

- http://www.convinceandconvert.com/social-media-measurement/the-5-key-2016-podcast-statistics/
- http://www.whypodcasts.org/audience/

SOCIAL MEDIA POSTS

Social media has completely transformed consumer and service provider interaction. It has put everyone on a level playing field: small businesses have as much clout as large corporations, and consumers have a direct, public channel of communication with the businesses they deal with.

Facebook, LinkedIn, Twitter, Instagram, Pinterest, Google +, YouTube – the list of social networking platforms goes on. Facebook alone has more than 1.7 billion active users around the globe.[2] If you want to educate your audience, generate sales and clinch more sales, it's a no-brainer: you need to be seen on social media.

In my work, I often meet people who feel overwhelmed by social media. They're hesitant to post their own content. I'm often told, "I don't know what to write. I don't want people to think I'm cocky or arrogant." Or, "What if people don't agree with what I post? What if they say negative things about me? I don't think I could cope!"

The tall poppy syndrome has a lot to answer for. In Australian culture, it's undesirable to stand out from the crowd. People shy away from the spotlight, fearing others will think they're egotistical. This fear extends to social media, where entrepreneurs choose the safe option of only sharing other people's content – or nothing at all.

---

[2] Facebook, http://newsroom.fb.com/company-info/

But your potential clients and existing customers *want* to hear from you. Figures from LinkedIn show that 6 out of every 10 of its users are interested in industry insights.[3] This means your audience wants to be educated about your area of expertise and perspective. LinkedIn goes on to say: "Your followers are active on LinkedIn because they want to be more productive and successful professionals. Informative, useful updates receive the highest engagement rates because that's the information members expect from companies they follow on LinkedIn."

Previously, only elite, invitation-only Influencers could post their own original content on LinkedIn. Now, anyone can. Yet only 15% of the 467 million people with a LinkedIn profile do. This represents an enormous opportunity for you to reach and educate your target audience.

To have maximum impact with social media, you need to take a three-dimensional approach. The following model explains how this works.

THREE-DIMENSIONAL SOCIAL MEDIA FOR EXPERTS

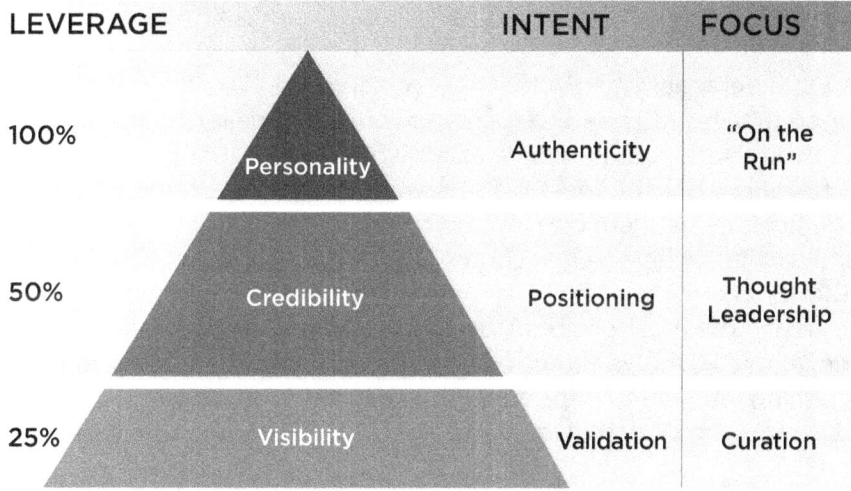

To establish an effective, three-dimensional social media strategy, you need to work your way through each of the following levels:

- **LEVEL 1: Visibility.** You're trying to establish a consistent online presence. You're focused on content **curation** – sharing the expertise of others to **validate** your own message and positioning. You're posting at least once a day to familiarise people with your face and your message. As an

---

[3] "7 Essential LinkedIn Marketing Stats: When to Post, What to Post and How to Improve." Buffer, March 24, 2014. https://blog.bufferapp.com/7-vital-statistics-to-help-with-your-linkedin-marketing-strategy

entrepreneur, these are two of your most important assets. However, it's important the information you share aligns with your message and your audience's needs. As US sales expert Harvey Mackay once said, "Don't confuse visibility with credibility." Visibility is about supporting your clients. Posting regular content doesn't necessarily mean you're educating or elevating your positioning. You must ensure the information you share is relevant to your audience and validates what you're saying. The amount of leverage you can receive from your social media strategy at this level is about 25% of what's possible.

- **LEVEL 2: Credibility.** Once you've established your visibility, you need to work on your credibility. Credibility is what gives your **positioning** its strength. Without credibility, everything you say and do is meaningless. In the words of American leadership expert John C. Maxwell, "Credibility is a leader's currency. With it, he or she is solvent. Without it, he or she is bankrupt." This level is about demonstrating that you're an authority in your industry. Sharing your own case studies, research and original ideas will cement your positioning as a **thought leader**. The amount of leverage you can receive at this level is about 50% of what's possible from your social media strategy.

- **LEVEL 3: Personality.** Now that you've achieved visibility and have proven your credibility, you need to focus on your personality. Sharing your personality with your audience establishes your **authenticity**. It gives you flavour and uniqueness. People want to see the person behind the message; it helps them connect with you more easily. In the words of Walt Disney, "Until a character becomes a personality, it cannot be believed ... Without personality, a story cannot ring true to the audience." At this top level, make the most of opportunities to share your personality **on the run**. For example, if you've attended an event, spoken at a conference or had something interesting happen to you that day, post about it! The amount of leverage you can receive at this level is 100% of what is possible.

Bear in mind that you can't skip straight from level 1 to level 3. Don't pressure yourself; take the time to master each level so you build a solid online presence. Only once you have built your visibility and credibility can you work on the personality of your social media strategy.

WHY CONTENT CURATION IS SO EFFECTIVE

Content curation is not only an efficient way for you to create social media posts, it bolsters your authenticity, too. Content creation is the process of collecting information relevant to your area of expertise and presenting it in a meaningful way. Compiling and sharing existing content from respected sources adds value for your followers. It shows them you genuinely want to educate them. It also adds weight to your own message. If someone else has said it, it's more trustworthy.

There are four main reasons why content curation works:

1. **It validates your message.** If you can show that other experts are saying what you're saying, your audience is more likely to trust and respect you.
2. **You can contrast your insights.** Sharing views you disagree with means you can add your own expertise and insights to the conversation.
3. **It's less salesy.** When you share other people's insights and research, you're less likely to come across as self-promoting in your posts.
4. **It's efficient.** You spend less time writing content, which means you can share more, add more value and increase your visibility.

THE IDEAL CONTENT RATIO

"You give before you get."
– Napoleon Hill

Content curation combined with your own thought leadership is a powerful combination. But you need to get the ratio right. The ideal content ratio is 80:20. That is, 80% of the content you share should be curated.

The remaining 20% should be your own original content. As an Influencer, you want to advance the thinking around your subject. But you don't want to over-expose your audience to your ideas. Limiting your own content to 20% of what you post reduces your risk of looking like a second-hand car dealer. You'll be able to highlight your offerings and educate your audience without making them feel as though they're being sold to all the time.

CREATE A CONTENT PLAN

A content plan is essential to keep your message on track. But you need to be clear about your goals to ensure your content plan is strategic. What do you want to sell this quarter? What are your goals for the next quarter? Plan your content around these goals.

It's a great idea to write your social media content 12 to 18 months in advance. All you need is a spreadsheet. If you don't plan, generating content each day becomes a real struggle. A solid content plan means you will know exactly what you need to say and when. When planning your content, there are several time-saving tools available to you. Scoop.it is a fabulous way to share content – and it's free. Once you set up your account, choose a word related to your area of expertise. For example, the word "resilience". Scoop.it will then send you a weekly email with links to articles it has found related to resilience. Use these links to create your social media posts.

POST FREQUENCY

How often should you post on social media? Finding the right balance can be tricky. On the one hand, if you post too often, you could irritate your audience. You'll clog up their newsfeeds and they'll unfollow you. On the other hand, if don't post enough, your audience will forget you. You'll lose traction with your personal brand and positioning. How can you get it just right?

The answer depends on several factors: the social media platform/s you're using, your industry, your business goals and your audience, to name a few. But there are some general rules of thumb you can use as a blueprint.

Social media-sharing platform Buffer suggests the following guide:[4]

- **Pinterest: 5 times per day.** Top brands have said they experience rapid growth by posting multiple times a day.
- **Twitter: 3 times per day.** Engagement slightly decreases after a third tweet.
- **Google +: 3 posts per day.** Posting consistently is key to keeping the level of traffic up.
- **Facebook and Instagram: 2 posts per day.** Any more than this and the number of likes and comments decreases.

Other research suggests you should only post twice a day on Facebook if you have at least 10,000 followers. If you post twice a day but have a smaller following, you'll receive 50% fewer clicks per post.[5] In this case, once a day is sufficient.

What about LinkedIn? Its own research has discovered that 20 posts per month can help you reach 60% of your unique audience.[6] This works out to be one post every weekday for four weeks. If you have the time and quality content, try scaling up your number of LinkedIn posts to reap more benefits.

---

[4] "Infographic: How Often Should You Post on Social Media? See the Most Popular Research and Tips." Buffer, February 2015, https://blog.bufferapp.com/how-often-post-social-media
[5] "How Frequently You Should Post on Social Media According to the Pros." *Forbes*, September 12, 2016, http://www.forbes.com/sites/neilpatel/2016/09/12/how-frequently-you-should-post-on-social-media-according-to-the-pros/#1743632a36d5
[6] "7 Essential LinkedIn Marketing Stats: When to Post, What to Post and How to Improve." Buffer, March 24, 2014, https://blog.bufferapp.com/7-vital-statistics-to-help-with-your-linkedin-marketing-strategy

THE VARIETY OF SOCIAL MEDIA PLATFORMS:

LINKEDIN

LinkedIn is a social network of more than 480 million people at all different levels in organisations, from CEOs to frontline staff, across a broad range of industries. It is a search algorithm based on networks and keywords. LinkedIn has created a complex algorithm of search tools and other platforms within it to enhance the experience. It also has an advertising platform.

LinkedIn is a little like an online resume, in that you can list your current and previous roles, create a blog, advertise a job and reach out to your ideal clients. According to LinkedIn:

- Professionals are signing up to join LinkedIn at a rate of more than two new members per second.
- There are more than 40 million students and recent college graduates on LinkedIn. They are LinkedIn's fastest-growing demographic.
- The most engaged LinkedIn users are white-collar workers, so it is ideal for business-to-business activity.

FACEBOOK

Facebook has more than 1.86 billion monthly active users as of December 31, 2016. As of April 2016, Facebook was the most popular social networking site in the world, based on the number of active user accounts.

Facebook is often used for business-to-consumer marketing activity. As a practice, you can have a personal page and a business page, with Facebook's marketing favouring business pages that pay for advertising.

Many business owners find Facebook's advertising platform complicated. It's easy to waste money with no results, so it's recommended that you seek the help of a Facebook advertising expert to help you.

TWITTER

Twitter posts, or tweets, are limited to 140 characters. Tweets are based on conversations and hash tags to make the content searchable. With only 140 characters to work with, it's a great way to learn how to be concise with your message!

Twitter has more than 313 million monthly users, and 82% are active users on mobile. Furthermore, 79% of Twitter accounts are based outside the United

States.[7] In recent years, Twitter has declined in popularity. It's trying to reinvent itself to keep up with changes to social media trends.

INSTAGRAM

Remember the phone book? It wasn't so long ago that when we needed a service or product, we'd pick up the phone book and search for a business that could help us.

In those days, the businesses that succeeded were the ones that had a name starting with "A". That's because they would be at the top of the A-Z listings. People would be more likely to call A-Plus Plumbers rather than W&W Plumbing Services.

But that's all changed. Phone books are a thing of the past. Forget A-Z listings – the businesses that succeed today are the ones that top social media feeds.

To be found, you need to be on social media. And one of the most powerful social media platforms is Instagram. It's the only social media platform that almost guarantees your profile a spot at the top of the feed. That's because Instagram has introduced a feature called Stories.

Stories brings your brand to life. It allows you to share and collate multiple photos and videos; all the moments of your day that combine to create your unique "story".

Videos are invaluable when it comes to building your personal brand. Gary Vaynerchuk, entrepreneur and master of social media, says spontaneous videos are an effective form of documentation. They capture your thoughts as they happen and help you collate your unique content – vital for any Influencer.

So, it's no surprise that Stories is proving to be a crucial brand-building tool for Influencers. Recent data shows that while Facebook has the highest number of members in Australia,[8] Instagram is the fastest-growing social network. Since Stories was launched in 2016, there's also been a decline in Snapchat usage[9] – previously the only social media platform that allowed users to post videos "on the run".

What's more, Instagram is driven by hashtags. This means it acts like a search

---

7 Twitter, https://about.twitter.com/company
8 "Social Media Statistics Australia – December 2016." *SocialMediaNews.com.au*, January 1, 2017, https://www.socialmedianews.com.au/social-media-statistics-australia-december-2016/
9 "Instagram's Stories is stealing Snapchat's users." *TechCrunch*, January 30, 2017, https://techcrunch.com/2017/01/30/attack-of-the-clone/

 JANE ANDERSON

engine, so you're more likely to turn up in search results when someone is looking online for a business like yours. It also uses location data, which is great news if you're targeting an audience in a specific area – for example, if you are a personal trainer in Brisbane.

There are two ways you can use Instagram to your advantage:

1. **As a polished branding tool.** Stylised images and videos can give your brand a refined edge.

2. **As a spontaneous capture tool.** Videos allow you to share the moments of your day as they happen. They give your audience a unique insight into who you are, what you do and how you can help them. It also shows them that you're a "real" person, not simply a message.

Negotiation expert Tony Perzow is a fantastic example of someone who uses Instagram videos in a powerful way. His videos not only market his programs, they inform, entertain and educate his audience. Wholehearted Studio's Hayley Jenkin is another entrepreneur who uses Instagram exceptionally well. Her images and videos are more stylised and consciously crafted, perfect for building her photography business's sophisticated brand.

Be wary, however, of striving for perfection. Entrepreneurs often have a fear of appearing inauthentic or "showy". Social media can be a real struggle for them, so they play it safe and do nothing. Consequently, their competitors appear at the top of their audiences' social media feeds. They're the ones who make an impact and get the leads.

Be fearless. To be an Influencer, you must embrace social media. Don't get hung up about appearing perfect – people want to see the real you. Videos can give you enormous cut through. Better yet, you don't need to spend huge amounts of money or have a professional recording studio. In this regard, Instagram presents the perfect ally.

SNAPCHAT

Snapchat is a photo and video-messaging app. Launched in 2011, Snapchat is unique in that all photos and videos last only a brief amount of time before they disappear forever. This makes the app ephemeral in nature, although you can take a screenshot of all the snaps you receive to save them in picture form. You can also save your own snaps before sending them to friends or your Story.

As of May 2014, the app's users were sending 700 million snaps a day. Due to the instant popularity of Snapchat, Facebook reportedly offered to acquire it for $3 billion.[10] But the cash offer was declined. Facebook later launched a similar app called Slingshot, but it failed to catch on.

Snapchat is mostly a hit among teenagers, according to several research firms, but it is catching on and being embraced by new demographics every day. Viners (people who create videos on Vine, a video-sharing app), YouTubers and celebrities are all known to use Snapchat as an alternative means of communicating with their followers.

BLOG

Blogging is a cost-effective, efficient way to educate people. It engages people with your brand and is essential for establishing your thought leadership.

Think of it as letting your potential clients take you for a test drive. We've all met the stereotypical car dealer who can only think of getting their commission. Before we buy, we need to get to know the car. We can't be hurried into a decision. We need to know if it's safe and economical. We need to know if it feels right. How do we do this? We take it for a spin.

Take your audience on a test drive into your world. Show them your insights and perspective. Give them a solid understanding of who you are and what you do. When written effectively, blog posts also act like a mirror: the reader sees themselves and their issues in what you're saying.

As an Influencer, you can't afford not to blog. Research shows that marketers who blog receive 67% more leads than those who do not.[11] Furthermore, 81% of US online consumers trust information and advice from blogs, and 61% of US online consumers have made a purchase based on recommendations from a blog.[12]

Regular blog posts are also a fantastic way of boosting your search engine optimisation (SEO). The more relevant content you have on your website, the more likely you will turn up in online search results. By using your targeted keywords in your blog posts and publishing consistently, you'll have a more viable online presence.

---

10 "Facebook Tried to Buy Snapchat for $3B in Cash. Here's Why." *Forbes*, November 13, 2013, https://www.forbes.com/sites/jeffbercovici/2013/11/13/facebook-wouldve-bought-snapchat-for-3-billion-in-cash-heres-why/#5526acd143de
11 "6 Stats You Should Know About Business Blogging in 2015." HubSpot, March 11, 2015.
12 "10 Important Reasons Why Entrepreneurs Need to Take Blogging Seriously." *Huffington Post*, July 13, 2016, http://www.huffingtonpost.com/jeff-charles/10-important-reasons-entr_b_10964854.html

WRITE VALUABLE CONTENT

To generate leads and drive customer action, your blog posts must add value. Your audience must walk away feeling as though they have learned something or gained an important insight. But sometimes when we are so close to our topic, we fail to look objectively at what we write.

How do you know if your content is adding value? According to *Forbes*, "if people seek it out, if people want to consume it, rather than avoiding it," then your content is valuable. The idea is to have people coming back for more. You want to create blog posts that people share and comment on.

To ensure the blog posts you write are engaging, educational and valuable, you need to:

1. **Be clear about your message and your audience.** It's surprising how many blogs out there have so much to say, yet fail to deliver a punchline. What's the point of what you're saying? What's your takeaway message? Who is your target audience and what do you want them to walk away with? How would you like them to act on the information you're giving them? Your message and your audience will also help you determine your tone of voice. Will your message have more impact if it's written in a conversational style? Or should it have a more instructional tone?

2. **Make it unique.** Don't regurgitate the same message everyone else is making. Offer something new. What do you have to say that no one else is saying? What makes you different? How can you get your message across by sharing your unique stories and perspective?

3. **Use images.** Enhance your content with photos, illustrations and infographics. The strategic use of images will not only break up the text and make your posts visually pleasing, they can help you emphasise a point and guide your readers though your ideas.

4. **Have a clear structure.** You're not writing a book, but blog posts still need structure. Without clearly organising your content, your message will get confused and your audience will stop reading. Use subheadings, bullet points and regular paragraph breaks to help with the flow of your content.

5. **Use links.** Hyperlink words or sentences that relate to other pages on your website. This not only boosts your SEO, it encourages readers to linger on your website for longer and consume more content.

And remember to always proofread your blog posts. Poor spelling and grammar detract from your message and undermine your position as a respected industry leader.

A good rule of thumb is to write your post, edit it, then wait 24 hours before you give it a final proofread. This gives you the clear headspace you need to detect errors that otherwise might have gone undetected in the rush to get it published.

CREATE A CALL TO ACTION

A call to action is the icing on the blog post cake. Essentially, it's a clickable link, button or image that prompts your readers to act. If you've given your readers informative, compelling content, by the time they reach the end of your post, they should feel inspired and motivated. Don't let them read and run. Ask them to act on their motivation.

Be clear and specific about your call to action. What would you like your audience to do? What is your objective? For example, you may want to build your client database. Provide a button that links to your e-newsletter opt-in form. If you have a book you want to sell, direct your audience to your shop. If you want readers to sign up to a workshop, create a button that links to your registration page.

Make your call to action as simple and clear as possible. Your readers will see it as the next logical step and will be more likely to click that button.

QUESTIONS FOR YOU TO CONSIDER:

1. What will you call your podcast? Who will be your ideal listener?

2. What topics will you talk about in the first 12 episodes?

3. When will you record your first six episodes so they're ready to upload when you launch your podcast?

4. Who will you be interviewing? When do you plan to reach out to them to ask if they will be on your show?

5. What script will you use to reach out so it saves you time rewriting for each episode?

6. What other ways can you leverage or re-purpose your podcast to create products for your customers?

CHAPTER 5.4

7. What questions will you ask them?

_____
_____
_____
_____

8. What social media platforms do your ideal customers hang out on?

_____
_____
_____

9. Which ones have you decided are best for your message and practice growth?

_____
_____
_____

10. If your ratio of curation and original content is 80:20, what content will you share for the next three months?

_____
_____
_____
_____

11. Which content-sharing tool will you use for your curation plan? Eg. Scoop.it? RSS feeds? Klout?

_____
_____
_____

12. What platform will you set up your blog in? When will you do this?

_____
_____
_____
_____

13. What are the topics for your first 12 blogs?

_____
_____
_____
_____

14. On what other platforms do you plan to share your blogs?

_____
_____
_____

15. What days and times do you have allocated in your calendar to write your blogs?

_____
_____
_____

16. Where do you plan to capture your blog ideas? (Hint: Set up a folder in your inbox or create a list in a Word document. Memo Mailer is also handy for capturing ideas.)

_____
_____
_____

17. Write down all the locations you will be in the next three weeks (the shops, the beach, cafe, airport). If you were to create a video on the run, what would the message be? For example, if you have a message about customer service, you could film it at your favourite coffee shop.

_____
_____
_____

18. What call to action will you put at the end of each blog post? For example, do you want people to attend your workshop? Buy your book?

_____
_____

CHAPTER 5.4

19. Which scheduling tool do you plan to use? Eg. Buffer, Hootsuite.

_____
_____
_____
_____

20. If you have decided to outsource this, who do you plan to use? What do you want them to do? Can you ask them for a sample of what they do before getting started?

_____
_____
_____
_____
_____

FROM HERE

We've covered everything you need to do to become an industry Influencer. When you're an industry Influencer, you have a greater impact on those you help – and the world.

If you have undertaken the Lead Generation Indicator, you will have identified the specific areas you need to grow your practice. Always start in the top right-hand corner with Direct Contact, then move out to the other activities in each quadrant.

Allocate time each day to work on those activities, whether it be reaching out to new people on LinkedIn, writing a blog or recording your podcast. How you spend your time creates your results. And the result, ultimately, is to become that industry leader.

It might seem there is a lot to do. And yes, ideally, you're building up to do all of these activities. You might not be able to do all of them at once, and some markets don't require all these activities.

Regardless, the key is to not feel overwhelmed. Undertake a bit at a time.

As Lao Tzu said, "A journey of a thousand miles begins with a single step."

"Our deepest fear is not that we are inadequate.

Our deepest fear is that we are powerful beyond measure.

It is our light, not our darkness that most frightens us.

We ask ourselves, Who am I to be brilliant, gorgeous, talented, and fabulous?

Actually, who are you not to be?

You are a child of God.

Your playing small does not serve the world.

There is nothing enlightened about shrinking so that other people will not feel insecure around you.

We are all meant to shine, as children do.

We were born to make manifest the glory of God that is within us.

It is not just in some of us; it is in everyone and as we let our own light shine, we unconsciously give others permission to do the same.

As we are liberated from our own fear, our presence automatically liberates others."

– Marianne Williamson

WANT MORE?

Jane Anderson is Australia's leading Personal Branding Expert. She speaks, mentors and runs workshops helping subject-matter experts become industry Influencers.

Jane writes her weekly blog and is featured in numerous magazines and media. To find out about Jane's other books, programs and workshops, go to www.jane-anderson.com, email support@jane-anderson.com or connect with Jane on the following social media platforms:

FACEBOOK
https://www.facebook.com/JaneAndersonPersonalBranding/

LINKEDIN
https://www.linkedin.com/in/janeandersonpersonalimpact/

INSTAGRAM
https://www.instagram.com/the_jane_anderson_/

TWITTER
@jane_anderson__

OTHER BOOKS BY JANE

CONNECT: Leverage Your LinkedIn Profile for Business Growth and Lead Generation in less than 7 Minutes Per Day

IMPACT: How to Build your Personal Brand for the Connection Economy

CONFIDENCE: Sell Yourself in Medical Interviews

www.ingramcontent.com/pod-product-compliance
Lightning Source LLC
Chambersburg PA
CBHW081138010526
44110CB00061B/2517